LETTERS TO THE SEVEN CHURCHES

Also by William Barclay in this series

Letters to the Seven Churches

William Barclay

Westminster John Knox Press
LOUISVILLE
LONDON •LEIDEN

Published in the U.S.A. in 2001 by
Westminster John Knox Press
Louisville, Kentucky

Original edition published in English under the title
Letters to the Seven Churches by John Hunt Publishing Ltd.,
46a West Street, New Alresford, Hants, UK.

PRINTED IN HONG KONG/CHINA

01 02 03 04 05 06 07 08 09 10 — 10 9 8 7 6 5 4 3 2 1

Library of Congress Cataloging-in-Publication Data
Barclay, William, 1907-1978.
  Letters to the seven churches / William Barclay.
    p. cm.
  Previously published: Philadelphia : Westminister Press, 1982.
  Includes index.
  ISBN 0-664-22386-9 (alk. paper)
  1. Bible. N.T. Revelation II-III--Criticism, interpretation, etc.
  2. Seven churches. I. Title.

BS2825.52.B37 2001
228'.06--dc2l

                                                  00-065479

Contents

Preface

The Book of the Revelation has always been regarded as largely unintelligible, and for that reason it has too often been abandoned by the general reader. The main aim of this book is to seek to show that the Book of the Revelation can become not only intelligible but highly relevant when the help of the available background material is brought to bear upon it.

The Book of the Revelation has been fortunate in its commentators, and he who writes upon it has many debts to acknowledge, for he must draw his material from many sources.

It is my hope that this book may do something to make the Letters to the Seven Churches, and indeed the whole Book of the Revelation, live for other preachers and for their congregations.

Trinity College,   WILLIAM BARCLAY
Glasgow

I
EPHESUS

The Vanity Fair of the Ancient World

The Book of the Revelation has suffered an unfortunate fate. On the whole it has either been abandoned by the readers of the Bible as being almost completely unintelligible, or it has become the happy hunting ground of religious eccentrics, who seek to construct from it a kind of celestial time-table of events to come. The obscurity of the Revelation has been felt by scholars in all ages. Jerome complained that the Revelation contained as many riddles as it does words. Luther would have banished it from the pages of the New Testament. He cited Revelation 1.3 and 22.18 where threats are made against the man who breaks the commandments of this book, and promises to the man who keeps them, and demanded how any man could possibly keep the commandments of a book which no man has even been able to understand. Still another scholar said that the Revelation either finds a man mad or leaves him so.

There is indeed much that is obscure and difficult in the Revelation, but there is one section of it at least which is vivid and relevant, and which gains much new light when it is set against the background out of which it was written. That is the section which contains the Letters to the Seven Churches, and it is these letters which we propose to study.

The first of the letters is addressed to the Church at Ephesus, and Ephesus was a city which had many a claim to greatness and to fame.

i. Ephesus was a city of the greatest commercial importance. In the ancient world communications were not as easy as they are today, and roads were neither as plentiful nor as good. The result was that trade tended to flow down river valleys, and thus a city set at the mouth of a river commanded the trade of the hinterland. Ephesus lay at the mouth of the river Cayster, and therefore it commanded the trade of the Cayster Valley. The course of the Cayster was short. It reached the narrow coastal plain between two ridges of mountains, and therefore it flowed fast. The consequence was that the harbor of Ephesus tended to silt up; but constant care and labor kept it open, and Ephesus was one of the greatest sea-ports of the ancient world.

Still further, three great roads converged on Ephesus. The great trade route from the Euphrates reached Ephesus by way of Colosse and Laodicaea, and brought the trade of the East to its markets. The road from Galatia came into Ephesus by way of Sardis, and poured into its lap the trade of Asia Minor. A third road came up from the south, and added the trade of the Maeander valley to the trade of the Cayster valley. Ephesus could fitly be called 'The Vanity Fair of the Ancient World'. In Revelation 18.12, 13 there is a magnificent list of merchandise: 'The merchandise of gold, and silver, and precious stones, and of pearls, and fine linen, and purple, and silk, and scarlet, and all thyine wood, and all manner vessels of ivory, and all manner vessels of most precious wood, and of brass, and iron, and marble, and cinnamon, and odors, and ointments, and frankincense, and wine, and oil, and fine flour, and wheat, and beasts, and sheep, and horses, and chariots, and slaves, and souls of men.' Farrar has suggested that that picture may well be drawn from the markets of Ephesus itself. In commerce and in wealth there were few cities to surpass Ephesus.

ii. Ephesus was a city of the greatest political importance. She enjoyed the title 'Supreme Metropolis of Asia'. It was what was known as a *free city*. That is to say that the Romans had granted to it the right of self-government within its own limits, and it never had the indignity of having Roman troops compulsorily quartered upon it. It had its own magistrates called *stratēgoi*; it had a democratically elected governing body called the *boulē*; it had an assembly of all its citizens called the *ekklēsia*. One of its main functionaries was called the *grammateus*. Acts 19.35 calls him the *town clerk*; but he was more than that. He kept the city archives; he introduced the business into the *boulē*; all correspondence to and from Ephesus passed through his hands; and he was present when money was deposited in the Temple of Diana.

Further, Ephesus was what was called an *assize town*. In Roman provinces there were certain centers where justice was dispensed. The Roman governor made regular and periodical tours throughout the provinces, and at these assize towns the governor tried the most important cases. So at certain times of the year Ephesus saw and reveled in all the pomp and pageantry of the arrival of the Roman governor and his staff. Ephesus well knew the grandeur that was Rome.

Still further, Ephesus was the center of the Pan-Ionian Games. Everyone knows the love of the Greek world for athletics and the Pan-Ionian ranked with the Olympic Games as athletic occasions. It was in the month of May that these games were held. The Greek name for that month was *Artemesion*, the month sacred to Artemis, which is the Greek name for Diana. At that time the whole population of Ionia flocked into Ephesus. There were public-spirited men who counted it an honor to make the arrangements for these games, and to bear the cost of them. These men were given the title *Asiarchs*, which means the Chiefs of Asia. They are referred to in Acts 19.31. To attain to such an office and such an honor was the high watermark of any man's career.

Ephesus was a city where men might look on the pageant and panorama of Graeco-Roman life at its most brilliant.

iii. Ephesus was a city of the greatest religious importance. Its greatest glory was the Temple of Diana. Ever since men had any record of history a temple had stood in Ephesus. The first temple is lost in the mist of antiquity. The second was built by the cities of Asia, aided by the wealth of Croesus, King of Lydia. It was burned down on the night that Alexander the Great was born. The third temple, the temple which was standing in the time of John, was one of the seven wonders of the world. The Greek saying ran: 'The sun sees nothing finer in his course than Diana's Temple.' It was the pride of Ephesus. When it was being built women gladly offered their jewels and their ornaments that it might be beautified. Alexander the Great had offered all the magnificent spoils of his eastern campaigns if only his name might be inscribed upon it; but his offer was refused, for none but the name of Ephesus might be connected with the Temple of Diana.

It was 425 feet long, 220 feet wide and 60 feet high. Only the center was roofed in. The great folding doors were made of cypress, and the roof of cedar wood. The stairway up to the roof was said to have been cut from one gigantic vine from the island of Cyprus.

The rest of the temple consisted of long pillared colonnades. There were 127 pillars, each of them the gift of a king. All of them were made of glittering Parian marble, and 36 of them were richly overlaid with gold and jewels and intricate carving.

In the inner shrine there stood the great altar, which had been carved by Praxiteles, the greatest of the Greek sculptors. Behind the altar there hung great draped velvet curtains. And behind the curtains there was the image of Diana. The image was so old that none knew whence it had come, and some said that it had fallen from heaven itself. It was not even certain of what it was made. Some said cypress wood, some cedar, some ebony, some the wood of the vine, some stone. To us the image would have come as distressingly disappointing. We think of Diana or Artemis as the loveliest of the goddesses, 'the huntress chaste and fair'. But the image was a black, squat, repulsive figure. It was covered with many breasts, which was the symbol of fertility, and held a club in one hand and a trident in the other. It was a strange, unlovely, uncouth figure, and on the base of it there were strange signs whose meaning no man knew. Yet to millions of people this strange image was the most sacred thing in the world.

Behind the image there was a still inner shrine. To it people came to deposit their valuables for safe-keeping. The Temple of Diana was in fact the Bank of England of the ancient world. In a world of wars and civil wars a temple was always a safe deposit, for seldom would a temple be violated, and the Temple of Diana was the safest of all.

The worship of the temple was a weird, ecstatic, hysterical business. To the accompaniments of shouts and wailings, the burning of incense and the playing on the flute, the worshippers worked themselves up into an emotional and hysterical frenzy in which the darkest and most shameless things could and did happen.

The priests were called *Megabyzi*. They were eunuchs. They were such because it was said that the goddess was so fastidious that she could bear no real male near to her; but there were those who said that they were such because the goddess was so lascivious that it was unsafe for any normal male to approach her. There were thousands of female priestesses called *Melissae*, which means the bees. There were hordes of slaves to sweep the courts and to undertake the menial duties of the temple. The Greek word for a temple sweeper is *neokoros*. And on its coins Ephesus called itself The *neokoros* of the Temple of Diana.

Proud city as it was, Ephesus was even prouder to call itself the most menial servant of Diana.

There were two further things connected with the Temple of Diana. The temple possessed the right of asylum. That is to say, if any man had committed a crime, if he could reach the precincts of the temple before he was arrested, he was safe. That immunity extended to an area one bowshot, or two hundred yards, all round the temple. It can easily be seen that the area around the Temple of Diana in Ephesus would house the choicest collection of criminals in the ancient world.

The temple was also the center of the sale of *Ephesian Letters*. These letters were charms. If a person wanted a safe journey, success in any enterprise, he would come to Ephesus and buy one of these Ephesian Letters. If a couple were childless and wished a child, if people were ill and could not be cured, these letters with their unintelligible words were considered to be the most powerful charms in the world. There was a story of a Greek wrestler at the Olympic Games who was invincible and who threw every opponent who faced him. It was discovered that he was wearing one of these Ephesian Letters tied to his ankle, and when that was removed – so it was said – he became as weak as any other man!

So into Ephesus there poured a stream of criminals of every kind, fugitives from the law, escapers and avoiders of justice, and into Ephesus there flowed a torrent of credulous, superstitious people, for in a superstitious world Ephesus was well-nigh the most superstitious city in the world.

iv. The character of the people of Ephesus was notoriously bad. The people had the reputation all over Asia of being fickle, superstitious and immoral. One of the most famous citizens of Ephesus was Heraclitus the philosopher. He was known throughout the world as the weeping philosopher and he was said never to smile. There exists a letter, which is spurious, but which purports to come from him. In it he is made to say that the darkness of the approach to the altar of the temple was the darkness of vileness; that the morals of the temple were worse than the morals of the beasts, for even promiscuous dogs do not mutilate each other. He said that the inhabitants of Ephesus were fit only to be drowned, and that the reason why he could never laugh or smile was because he lived amidst such terrible uncleanness.

Such was Ephesus. It was there that Paul stayed longer than he did in any other city, and it was there that some of the greatest victories of grace were won. Sometimes we say that it is hard to be a Christian in a modern, industrial, competitive civilization. Let us remember Ephesus, and let us remember that there were Christians there.

II
EPHESUS

The Church which left its First Love

John begins by calling the Risen Christ the one WHO HOLDS THE SEVEN STARS IN HIS HAND, AND WHO WALKS IN THE MIDST OF THE SEVEN GOLDEN CANDLESTICKS. There is an interesting and illuminating grammatical point in the Greek of this sentence. The SEVEN STARS and the SEVEN CANDLESTICKS both stand for the seven Churches. The Greek verb for TO HOLD is *kratein*, which is normally followed by a genitive of that which is held. The genitive case is the case which in English we express by the word *of*; *of the book* is the genitive case. The reason for this genitive case is that when we take hold of something, if it is a large thing, we take hold, not of the whole of it, but of part of it. When, for instance, I take hold of a normal sized book, it is only part of the book that I actually hold within my hand. When *kratein* does take an accusative, which is the case of the direct object, it means *to hold the whole of an object within one's hand*. For instance, I would hold the whole of a hazel nut within my hand, and that would be expressed by *kratein* with the direct accusative.

In this sentence *kratein* is used, not with the usual genitive, but with the much more unusual accusative. The meaning is that Jesus Christ holds *the whole of the Church* within His hand. It is not any one Church which belongs exclusively to Jesus Christ;

no single Church is the Church of Christ. He holds *all the Churches* in His hand, for all the Churches are His and all belong to Him.

Further, HE WALKS IN THE MIDST OF THE SEVEN GOLDEN CANDLESTICKS. That is to say the presence of the Risen Christ is in every Church. His presence and His power are not confined to any one Church; He is there in the midst of them all.

So long as we think of *our* Church, *our* constitution, *our* method of church government there can be nothing but disunity and disintegration. The only way to real union of all the Churches is to think of the Risen Christ who holds *all* the Churches in His hand and who is in the midst of *all* of them. To achieve real unity within the Churches and among the Churches we must ever think of the Christ who unites, and forget the human things which divide.

In verses 2-4 John singles out three things about the Church in Ephesus.

i. It is a Church which has Christian *energy*. In verse 2 he writes: I KNOW THY WORKS, AND THY LABOR, AND THY PATIENCE. The first *and* in that sentence is a special kind of *and*. It is called in Greek *the epexegetic and*. It does not simply *add* something to that which goes before, as if it were adding another item to a list in a catalog; it *explains* what has gone before. The correct translation would be: I KNOW THY WORKS – BY THAT I MEAN YOUR LABOR AND YOUR PATIENCE. Both LABOR and PATIENCE are great and notable words.

The Greek word *for labor* is *kopos*, and *kopos* means *the toil which exhausts*. The Church is not the place for the dilettante; it is the place for the man who is willing to sweat, willing to toil till he drops for the sake of the work of Jesus Christ.

The Greek word for *patience* is *hupomonē*. *Hupomonē* is not the patience which sits down and passively bears things, the patience which allows a tide of troubles to sweep over its bowed head. The word would be better translated *triumphant fortitude*. Someone once said to a person who was suffering terribly: 'Suffering colors life, doesn't it?' Back came the answer: 'Yet, but I propose to choose the color.' When Beethoven's terrible deafness descended upon him, blotting out the world of lovely sounds which to a musician is everything, he said: 'I will take life by the throat.' Once my father went to see a girl who had had a long illness and who was quite helpless. She would never walk again, and all that she had to look forward to was a slow and lingering death. He took with him a little book of Christian comfort, a book radiant with certainty and with joy. He gave it to her, saying: 'I thought that you might like to have this book.' She took it and looked at it and smiled. Then she said shyly: 'I wrote it.' All these things are *hupomonē*. *Hupomonē* is not simply the patience which accepts and submits, although such acceptance and submission are a necessary beginning. *Hupomonē* is what has been called that 'masculine constancy under trial', that triumphant fortitude which can transmute suffering into glory.

ii. It is a Church which has preserved Christian *orthodoxy*. It has tested those which are apostles, and which are not, and has branded the latter as liars. The Church at Ephesus could discern between the true and the false teachers. There is only one acid test of any teacher – and that is likeness to Jesus Christ. A child was once in a hospital at Christmas time, and on Christmas day a Christmas service was held in the ward. The story of Jesus was sweetly and wisely and winsomely told. The child came from a home where she had been taught nothing about these things, and where she had never before heard the story of the Christian joy. After the service the child said to a nurse, who – unlike most nurses – was a curiously acidulated creature: 'Did you ever hear that story about this man Jesus before?' 'O, yes,' said the nurse, 'often.' 'Well,' said the child, 'you certainly don't look like it.' The terrible test which every teacher must undergo is likeness to Christ.

iii. The Church at Ephesus had two great qualities. It had Christian *energy* in plenty; it preserved Christian *orthodoxy* with care. But it lacked one thing; and that lack undid all the good the other virtues might have done. The Church at Ephesus lacked Christian *love*. The Risen Christ said sadly: I HAVE SOMEWHAT AGAINST THEE, BECAUSE THOU HAST LEFT THY FIRST LOVE. This sentence may have two possible meanings; or, in this case it may well not be a case of *either or*, for both meanings may be there.

(*a*) It has already been said that the Church at Ephesus could not bear false teaching. It may be that the Church at Ephesus was so busy heresy-hunting that it had lost the atmosphere of brotherly love. It may be that a hard, censorious, critical, fault-finding, stern self-righteousness had banished the spirit of love. H. B. Swete writes on this passage: 'Patience and unremitting toil in His cause are not all that Christ requires, and, indeed, are of little value, if love be absent.' Strict orthodoxy can cost too much, if it has to be bought at the price of love.

(*b*) It may mean that the first enthusiasm of the Christian faith was gone, that the honeymoon period was over, that 'the love of thine espousals' (Jeremiah 2.2) was only a memory. That can happen to anyone. How can we avoid that fading of enthusiasm, that failure of love? We can do so in two ways. First, we can do it by constantly reminding ourselves of what Jesus Christ has done for us. John Newton came the long way round to Christ. He had plumbed the depths when he was a slave-trader upon the high seas. When he was a converted man, he wrote a text in great letters and hung it above his mantelpiece: 'Thou shalt remember that thou wast a bondman in the land of Egypt, and the Lord thy God redeemed thee.' F.

W. Boreham quotes a letter which Thomas Goodwin, the Puritan preacher, wrote to his son: 'When I was theatening to become cold in my ministry, and when I felt Sabbath morning coming, and my heart not filled with amazement at the grace of God, or when I was making ready to dispense the Lord's Supper, do you know what I used to do? I used to take a turn up and down among the sins of my past life, and I always came down with a broken and a contrite heart, ready to preach, as it was preached in the beginning, the forgiveness of sins.' We shall not lose the glow, if we take as our motto: 'I will not forget what He did for me.' Second, we can do it by living close to Jesus Christ. Friendship will die unless it is nourished by continual contact. 'A man, sir,' said Dr Johnson, 'should keep his friendship in constant repair.' If there is never a day when we do not seek the presence of the Risen Lord, the love of Him will never fade.

In verse 5 there are the three great imperatives of the Christian life – REMEMBER, REPENT, DO. We must ever *remember* what our sins cost God. To quote Goodwin again: 'Many a Sabbath morning, when my soul had been cold and dry for the lack of prayer during the week, a turn up and down in my past life before I went into the pulpit always broke my hard heart, and made me close with the gospel for my own soul before I began to preach.' We must never lose the memory of what we have done to God, and what God has done for us. We must REPENT. There must be in our hearts neither defiance nor indifference, but a godly sorrow for our sins. We must DO. The only thing that a man can do to demonstrate the reality of his repentance is to live in newness of life. The sorrow of true repentance is not an emotion in which we luxuriate, but an antiseptic which cleanses our lives.

Failure to bring about this change means THE REMOVAL OF THE CANDLESTICK FROM ITS PLACE, that is to say, the rejection of the Church. The duty of the Church is to be the light of the world, to shine like a light in a dark place. When an electric light bulb loses its power to shine, we throw it away, because it has lost the power of doing what it was created to do. Uselessness always invites disaster, and the Church which has ceased to shine for Christ has lost the reason for its existence.

Verse 6 speaks about THE DEEDS OF THE NICOLAITANS. The Nicolaitans were said to be the heretical followers of Nicolas of Antioch, who was one of the chosen seven (Acts 6.5). It was said that Nicolas went wrong and ended in heresy. It has been very probably suggested that the Nicolaitans are the same people as the people in Pergamos who followed the teaching of Balaam (verse 14). *Nicolas* could be derived from the two Greek words *laos*, which means *the people*, and *nikan*, which means *to conquer*. *Balaam* could be derived from the Hebrew words *am* and *baal*, which mean exactly the same two things. The two names could be the same, one in Greek and one in Hebrew. If that be so, the faults of the two sets of heretics are the same.

The error of those who followed the doctrine of Balaam was that they taught the people TO EAT THINGS SACRIFICED UNTO IDOLS, AND TO COMMIT FORNICATION (verse 14). These were the very two things which all agreed not to do when the Gentiles were accepted into the Christian Church at the Council of Jerusalem (Acts 15.20). The Nicolaitans were very likely people who said that the Christian is freed from all law, and that he can do exactly what he likes. They perverted the teaching of Paul, and turned Christian liberty into Christian licence.

The worst things are always the corruption of the best. It is true that the Christian possesses perfect liberty. But the Christian can never do what *he* likes; he must always do what *God* likes. As it has been put: 'Love God and do what you like.' But when we really and truly love God, we will never do anything which either grieves God or hurts our fellowmen.

Christian liberty is not freedom to please ourselves; it is freedom from self and sin and Satan in order that we may please God.

In verse 7 John says: HE THAT HATH AN EAR TO HEAR, LET HIM HEAR WHAT THE SPIRIT SAITH TO THE CHURCHES. It is as if John said: 'This letter is addressed to the whole Church at Ephesus, but *this means you.*' We must always remember that every promise and every command of the Bible is offered and addressed personally to us. Henry Ward Beecher once said: 'The Churches of the land are sprinkled all over with baldheaded old sinners whose hair has been worn off by the constant friction of countless sermons that have been aimed at them and glanced off and hit the man in the pew behind.' When we hear God's truth, it is our duty to apply it, not to other people, but to ourselves.

The final promise to the man who overcomes is that the Risen Christ WILL GIVE HIM TO EAT OF THE TREE OF LIFE, WHICH IS IN THE MIDST OF THE PARADISE OF GOD. The Jewish Rabbis taught that in Paradise the tree of life would be there in the middle of heaven, and that all might eat of it. The tree of life is the symbol of immortality, and the meaning of the promise is that, if we live victoriously in the power of the Risen Christ, we have in us the medicine of salvation, the power which defeats death and gives us eternal life.

III
SMYRNA

The Glory of Asia

Smyrna was a very ancient and a very great city, and to this day Smyrna is a city of 250,000 inhabitants. Smyrna was one of the very few Churches to which the Risen Christ gave unqualified and unalloyed praise, and it is of interest to note that to this day half the population of Smyrna is Christian, and Smyrna is one of the great centers of learning and piety of the Eastern Orthodox Church. Smyrna had many claims to distinction.

i. Smyrna was a great trade city. It stood on a deep gulf thirty-five miles to the north of Ephesus. It had a magnificent harbor, rendered all the more valuable by the fact that it could be totally enclosed in time of war. Smyrna stood at the end of the road which served the valley of the river Hermus, and all the trade of that valley flowed into its markets and found an outlet through its harbor. It had a specially rich trade in wines. Smyrna, like Ephesus, was a city of wealth and of commercial greatness.

ii. Smyrna was an outstandingly beautiful city. It claimed to be *to agalma tēs Asias*, the Glory of Asia. It had been built in the fourth century B.C. and it was a model of all that town-planning should be. Great, straight, spacious streets ran from one end of the city to the other. The most famous of these streets was called the Golden Street. At the sea end of it there stood the Temple of Cybele; on the way along it there were temples to Apollo, to

Asklepios and to Aphrodite; and inland, where the street met the foothills, there stood the Temple of Zeus. The Christians in Smyrna lived in a situation in which on every side the splendors of heathen worship met their eyes. What a contrast there was between their humble meeting places and the glory of the temples of the gods of Greece!

Smyrna possessed a famous stadium and an equally famous library. It claimed to possess the largest public theater in Asia Minor. One of her most famous monuments was a monument to Homer, whose birthplace it claimed to be.

It would have been easy for the little Christian Church in Smyrna to have been stifled and suffocated out of existence by the weight of the heathen splendor which surrounded it, but it is blessedly true that not all the darkness in the world can quench the smallest light, when that light had been kindled and is constantly nourished by God.

iii. Politically Smyrna was an important city. In all the civil wars it had chosen the right side, and the Romans had not forgotten to be grateful. Smyrna was a free city and an assize town.

Smyrna was by no means unconscious of its own greatness. It was said to be the most municipally proud of all the cities of Asia Minor. Mommsen called it 'a paradise of municipal vanity'. It claimed to be the first in beauty; it claimed to be the first in Caesar worship; it claimed to be the birthplace of Homer. Smyrna would look with contempt on poor and humble Christians, and would despise them as of no importance. To Smyrna earthly honors were 'the first and the last', not God.

iv. Smyrna had two characteristics which made life for the Christians a constant and continued peril. Smyrna was one of the great centers of Caesar worship. If we are to understand the peril and the threat which was at the back of every Christian life when the Book of the Revelation was written, we must understand how Caesar worship arose and how it functioned.

The problem of Rome was how to unify its vast Empire. The Roman Empire was a vast conglomeration of states and cities and nations and peoples and races covering the whole known world. Something was needed to unify and to integrate all the varying elements in this huge mass. None of the extant religions was capable of being universalized. But one thing was capable of being universalized – the spirit of Rome itself. It is not to be thought that the provincials resented Roman government. More than one king had deliberately willed his kingdom into the possession of Rome. The provincials owed much to Rome, and they knew it. Under the sway of Rome men enjoyed the *pax Romana*, the Roman peace. Life which had once been a perilous business flowed peacefully on. Goodspeed writes: 'This was the *pax Romana*, the Roman peace. The provincial under Roman sway found himself in a position to conduct his business, provide for his family, send his letters, and make his journeys in security, thanks to the strong hand of Rome.' The seas were cleared of pirates; the great Roman roads were cleared of brigands. Men no longer lived under the capricious rule of unaccountable despots and tyrants, but under the control of strict and impartial Roman justice. It was not difficult to turn the spirit of Rome into a power which men were gratefully willing to worship. So was born the worship of *Dea Roma*, the goddess Rome.

At first this was a spontaneous and a voluntary affair, and at first it was largely confined to the East. But it went further. There was a vagueness about the conception of the spirit of Rome; but there was one person who incarnated and embodied that spirit, and that one man was the Emperor. In him the spirit of Rome assumed a visible form. So Emperor worship arose. The early emperors deprecated this worship, and even shrank from it. But the movement which had begun so spontaneously could not be halted; first the worship was accepted; and then it was officialized and the emperor was officially created a god.

But the matter was to go even further than that. Here was the very thing which could unite the varied mass which constituted the Roman Empire. Emperor worship had begun as spontaneous demonstration of gratitude to Rome; but towards the end of the first century, in the days of Domitian, the final step was taken and *Caesar worship became compulsory*. Once a year the Roman citizen must burn a pinch of incense on the altar to the godhead of Caesar; and, having done so, he was given a certificate to guarantee that he had performed his religious duty. We possess a request for and a specimen of such a certificate. The request runs:

> To those who have been appointed to preside over the sacrifices, from Inares Akeus, from the village of Theoxenis, together with his children Aias and Hera, who reside in the village of Theadelphia. We have always sacrificed to the gods, and now, in your presence, according to the regulations, we have sacrificed and offered libations, and tasted the sacred things, and we ask you to give us a certification that we have done so. May you fare well.

The certificate itself runs:

> We, the representatives of the Emperor, Serenos and Hermas, have seen you sacrificing.

Then follows the date. Every Roman citizen had to make that sacrifice and receive that certificate.

One thing is clear. The burning of this pinch of incense was obviously not a test of a man's religious orthodoxy; it was a test of his political loyalty. In point of fact the Roman government was extremely tolerant. Once a man had made his sacrifice and received his certificate, he could go and worship any god or goddess he liked, provided that worship did not conflict with public decency and order. But if he refused to burn that pinch of incense, he was by his refusal automatically branded as a disloyal and disaffected citizen. With an Empire the size of the Roman Empire, no government could afford to have disaffected citizens, who might become stormcenters of trouble. Therefore any man who refused to burn his pinch of incense was rendered by his very refusal an outlaw.

All that the Christians had to do was to burn that pinch of incense, say, 'Caesar is Lord', receive their certificate and go away and worship as they pleased. But that is precisely what the Christians would not do. They would give to no man the name of Lord; that name they would keep for Jesus Christ and Jesus Christ alone. They would not even formally conform. Uncompromisingly the Christians refused to go through the forms of Caesar worship, and therefore the Christians were outlaws, and liable to persecution at any time. Persecution was not continuous, but it was liable to break out at any time, for informers were frequent and numerous. The Christian was like a man over whose head the sword of execution was constantly poised, and he never knew when it might fall, for the Roman government regarded his refusal to conform as the act of a dangerous and disloyal citizen.

Nowhere can life have been more dangerous for a Christian than in Smyrna. As far back as 196 B.C. Smyrna had been the first city in the world to erect a temple to Dea Roma, the goddess Rome. In A.D. 26 Smyrna strove with six other cities of Asia Minor for the right to erect a temple to the godhead of Tiberius, the reigning Emperor, and won it. Smyrna was an enthusiastic center of Caesar worship. For a man to become a Christian anywhere was to become an outlaw. In Smyrna, above all places, for a man to enter the Christian Church was literally to take his life in his hands. In Smyrna the Church was a place for heroes.

v. We have said that there were two things in Smyrna which were ever-present threats to the Christians. The second was that in Smyrna there was a very large Jewish population. Again and again it was the Jews who informed against the Christians, or who gained the ear of the local governor and incited him to unleash an attack of persecution upon the Christians. The Jews stuck at nothing in their attempts to obliterate the Christian Church.

In the later days it was in Smyrna that the Jews were responsible for one of the most famous martyrdoms in history, the martyrdom of Polycarp, the bishop of Smyrna. It was a festival day, and the crowds were in a highly excitable and inflammable state. The cry went up to seize Polycarp the Christian bishop. He freely confessed that he was a Christian. He was given the choice – worship the godhead of Caesar, or die. The Jews led the shouts of the mob: 'This is the teacher of Asia, the father of the Christians, the destroyer of the gods, who teaches many neither to offer sacrifice nor to worship.' Polycarp was given the choice – sacrifice to Caesar or be burned. He gave his immortal answer: 'Eighty and six years have I served Christ, and He has never done me wrong. How can I blaspheme my King who saved me?' It was the Sabbath day, and yet the Jews were foremost in gathering faggots for the fire, thereby breaking their own Sabbath law. 'It is well,' said Polycarp, 'I fear not the fire that burns for a season, and after a while is quenched. Why do you delay? Come, do your will.' As the flames licked his body, he prayed his great prayer: 'I thank Thee that Thou hast graciously thought me worthy of this day and of this hour, that I may receive a portion in the number of the martyrs, in the cup of Thy Christ.' And so Polycarp died, and it was the Jews who were behind his death.

The Jews were strong in Smyrna; they had the ear of the authorities. Such was their envenomed bitterness that they would even plead concern for the pagan gods, and even join with the hated Gentiles, if by so doing they could bring death to the Christians. It was a threat like that which in Smyrna hung over the Christian Church.

There were Christians in Smyrna who were men of such heroic calibre that the word of the Risen Christ to them was a word of unadulterated praise. In a city where the splendor of heathen worship might well have suffocated the life out of the Christian Church, in a city where the pride of men looked on the humble Christians with arrogant contempt, in a city where every Christian was between the devil of the demands of Caesar worship and the deep sea of Jewish slander and malignancy, there were Christians who were faithful unto death.

IV
SMYRNA

Faithful unto Death

REVELATION 2.8-11

This letter begins in verse 8 with two great titles of the Risen Christ. The Risen Christ is called THE FIRST AND THE LAST. Here was something which could indeed lift up the hearts of the Christians of Smyrna. They were in dire peril. The demands of Caesar worship and the malignant slanders of the Jews could at any time make life an agony; but, no matter what happened, in any possible situation, from before the beginning to after the end of time, the Risen Christ was with them.

In the old days, when much of the world was unexplored and unknown, and when many lands were lands of mystery, men drew their maps; and in the unknown places they wrote such things as, 'Here be dragons', 'Here be burning fiery sands'. The Christian can take the map of life and write across every part of it, 'Here is Christ'.

When a man realizes that great truth, there enters into his life a new security. Nothing unbearable can happen to him, if he can never be separated from Jesus Christ. When Rupert Brooke went out to battle in the days of the first World War, he wrote in his poem *Safety*:

> Safe shall be my going,
> Secretly armed against all death's endeavor;
> Safe though all safety's lost; safe where men fall;
> And if these poor limbs die, safest of all.

John Greenleaf Whittier wrote with the same confidence:

> I know not where His islands lift
>   Their fronded palms in air;
> I only know I cannot drift
>   Beyond His love and care.

It was exactly the same certainty of which Paul wrote lyrically when he made a list of all the terrible and the threatening things in a perilous universe, and then declared that there was nothing in heaven or earth which could separate him from the love of God in Jesus Christ his Lord (Romans 8.38, 39).

The second title of the Risen Christ with which this letter begins is the title HE WHO WAS DEAD AND IS ALIVE AGAIN. The Greek verb which the Authorized Version translates *is alive* is not a present tense, as that translation might make us think. It is an aorist, and the aorist in Greek expresses one definite, completed act in past time. A better translation would therefore be, HE WHO WAS DEAD AND CAME TO LIFE AGAIN. The reference is to *the event of the Resurrection*. The threat of death at any moment hung poised over every Christian in Smyrna, and it must have been an uplifting thing to remember that always with them there was one who had conquered death, one who had taken on the last enemy and who had shattered his power.

This double title of the Risen Christ means that in life there is with us one from whom no time and no event can ever separate us, and that in death there is one with us who conquered death. Of whom then shall we be afraid?

Verse 9 tells of the troubles which the Christians at Smyrna had to face and to suffer.

i. There was TRIBULATION. The Greek word is *thlipsis*, which means *pressure*; and in classical Greek it is always used in its literal sense. It is, for instance, used of a man who was tortured to death by being slowly crushed by a great boulder laid upon him. In life there is always pressure. H. G. Wells wrote in his autobiography: 'Most individual creatures, since life began, have been up against it. ... They have had to respond to the unresting antagonism of their circumstances.' There is the pressure of work, the pressure of worry, the pressure of material circumstances, the pressure of opposition and antagonism and persecution. Under that pressure many people collapse. Life becomes too much for them; physically and mentally they cannot stand the strain.

It is there that Christ comes in. G. K. Chesterton said that it was the sign of a real man that he could pass the breaking-point, and not break. When God spoke to Ezekiel, He said: 'Son of man, *stand on thy feet*, and I will speak unto thee; and the Spirit entered into me, when He spoke unto me, *and set me upon my feet*' (Ezekiel 2.1, 2). To put it in our modern idiom, Jesus Christ enables us to cope with life, to meet the pressures of life erect and on our feet.

ii. There was POVERTY. The word which is here used for poverty is *ptōcheia*, which means, not so much *poverty*, as *destitution*. In Greek there are two words for poverty. *Penia* describes the poverty of the man who has to work for his living; it describes the poverty of the man who has nothing superfluous; but *ptōcheia* describes the poverty of the man who has nothing at all. As far as worldly possessions went, the Christians of Smyrna were destitute, but they had *God*. There are three things which we may here note.

(*a*) Generally speaking the early Christians were poor (I Corinthians 1.26, 27; James 2.5). When Jesus chose his twelve disciples, in effect He said: 'Give me twelve ordinary men and I will change the world.' When the most ordinary person finds contact with Christ, he is clad with a new dignity, which is not his own. God does not so much need extraordinary people as He needs ordinary people whom He can fill with His power so that they can do extraordinary things.

(b) Smyrna was one of the wealthiest of cities, and yet the Christians were poor to the point of destitution. We do well to remember that the gap between the two ends of the social scale is no new thing. Plato said that every city is two cities, the city of the rich and the city of the poor, and that there is a constant civil war between them. Pliny tells us that he saw a Roman bride whose dress was to bedecked with gems and jewels that it was worth $600,000; and at the very same moment the poor people of Rome were starving, because gales had delayed the corn ships from Alexandria, and the corn doles were late in being distributed. The difference between the modern world and the ancient world is that the ancient world accepted that situation as being in the nature of things. Aristotle said that there were many men who were born to be slaves, hewers of wood and drawers of water, men whose sole reason for existence was that they might slavishly do the menial duties for the upper classes. One of the great practical effects of Christianity has been, not that that situation has been wholly cured, but that men have come to see at least that it is wrong to live in a civilization where that great gap exists. It is at least true that since Christianity came men have refused to accept this situation as being in the nature of things.

(c) It is very probably true that the Christians of Smyrna were, at least in some cases, poor because their homes had been deliberately pillaged and plundered. The writer to the Hebrews wrote to his people: 'You received the pillaging of your home with joy' (Hebrews 10.34). It was dangerous to be a Christian in the ancient world. It is not safe yet, for in many cases it is a fact that, if a man insisted on carrying his Christian principles into his business life or into his everyday life, he would be in very real danger of losing his job.

iii. The Christians were always in danger because of the blasphemy of the Jews. The word which is translated blasphemy is the Greek word *blasphēmia*. It would be better to translate it *slander*. In the ancient world in many cases the Jews had the ear of those in high places. This was particularly true because many women were attracted by the high moral tone and the sexual purity of Judaism. The Jews could easily influence such women to influence their husbands. Nero was the first persecutor of the Christians. His favorite actor Aliturus, and his infamous harlot Empress Poppaea were both Jewish proselytes, and there is little doubt that it was their slanderous and perverted information which turned Nero against the Christians. The Jews whispered their slanders against the Christians into the ears of the Roman authorities with calculated and poisonous venom. James Drawbell, the famous journalist, has a sentence or two in one of his books: 'I admire conscientious objectors in this war, so long as they are conscientious; and I admire soldiers. The only ones I never admire are the ones who fight with their mouths.' To fight with one's mouth is always contemptible. The slanderer and the malicious gossip have much to answer for – and they will answer for it.

The Risen Christ calls the Jewish Synagogue THE SYNAGOGUE OF SATAN. The full and official title of the Synagogue was *The Synagogue of the Lord*. But in some cases the religion of the Jews had become so perverted that the Synagogue was no longer the house of God, but the home of the devil. Once John Wesley was speaking to someone who had a cruel and perverted idea of religion. 'Your God,' he said, 'is my devil.' When a man refuses to listen to God, he is always certain to begin listening to the devil.

In verse 10 we see the honesty of Jesus Christ. He never offered His people an easy way; He offered them suffering, imprisonment and trial. No one can ever say that he was induced to follow Christ on false pretences. W. R. Maltby once said that Christ promised His people three things – that they would be in constant trouble; that they would be completely fearless; and that they would be absurdly happy.

The phrase TEN DAYS is not to be taken literally; it is the normal Greek phrase for a short time.

In verse 10 we have the famous phrase A CROWN OF LIFE. The Greek word is *stephanos*. It is to be noted that in Greek *stephanos* is not the royal crown; that is *diadēma*, from which the English word *diadem* comes. *Stephanos* has three main usages.

i. It is the crown of victory in the games, the wreath of laurel which was given to the athlete who overcame. The Christian is the athlete of God. The race may be long and hard; it may take all that a man has to give. The Christian is the man who is for ever pressing towards a goal. But the end of the struggle makes it worth it all.

ii. It is the festal crown which was worn at marriages and on other festal occasions. The Christian life is a life of joy now, and joy hereafter.

iii. In Smyrna this word *stephanos* would have both these meanings but it would have another meaning also. In Smyrna the reward for faithful municipal service was a laurel crown. On the coins of Smyrna it is common to see great and honored magistrates so depicted and so crowned. If the Christian is to receive his reward, he must be faithful in the service of his fellowmen. He is in this world to serve.

In verse 11 there comes the final promise that the man who overcomes will not be HURT OF THE SECOND DEATH. *The second death* was a Jewish Rabbinic phrase for *the total extinction of the utterly wicked*. The idea behind this phrase, as it is used here, is that fidelity to Christ may bring death on earth, but it brings life in eternity. Infidelity may save a man's life on earth, but in the end it brings something far worse; it brings the death of the soul. The man who is faithful unto death dies to live; but the man who saves his life at the cost of principles and at the price of his loyalty to Christ lives to die.

V
PERGAMOS

The Most Illustrious City of Asia

The road from Ephesus led north along the sea coast for about forty miles; then it turned inland to the north-east; and fifteen miles inland, in the valley of the Caicus, stood the city of Pergamos. One special fact marked out Pergamos from all the other neighboring cities; Pergamos was a capital city; and a capital city has an air and atmosphere all its own. London and Edinburgh, Paris and Berlin, have this feeling which only a capital city can have. From 231 B.C. to 133 B.C. Pergamos had been the capital of the Attalid kingdom, which was one of the parts into which the empire of Alexander the Great broke up. In 133 B.C. its dying king had willed it into the possession of the Roman Empire. Pergamos had become part of the Roman Empire, not by unwilling conquest and compulsion, but by spontaneous choice. The Romans made her the capital of the province of Asia, and that honor she retained down to A.D. 130. So then when John wrote his letter Pergamos had been a capital city for more than three hundred years.

Pergamos could never attain the commercial eminence and the commanding trade position of Ephesus or Smyrna; its geographical position forbade that. But though it was inferior in trade it was far superior to them in historical greatness. Pergamos was historically the greatest city in Asia Minor. Pliny, the Roman writer, called her *longe clarissimum Asiae*, by far the most famous city of Asia. Pergamos had all the atmosphere of an ancient capital city, and all the pride of centuries of greatness behind her.

Pergamos had certain very definite claims to fame which all the world knew.

i. Pergamos had one of the most famous libraries in the world. It contained no fewer than two hundred thousand books, an immense number in an age when every book had to be written and copied by hand. So close was the connection of Pergamos with literary activity that the word *parchment* is in fact derived from the name *Pergamos*; and behind that derivation there lies a tale. *Parchment*, or, as it is sometimes called, *vellum*, was a writing material made from the skins of animals. It is on it that all the great New Testament manuscripts are written. Its original name was *hē Pergamēnē charta*, which means the Pergamene sheet, and is the expression from which the word *parchment* is derived. Prior to the invention and manufacture of parchment the main writing material was *papyrus*, which was manufactured from the pith of a bulrush which grew almost exclusively on the banks of the Nile. In Egypt the manufacture of papyrus was a government monopoly, a kind of nationalized industry. At the time when parchment was invented Eumenes was king of Pergamos and Ptolemy was king of Egypt. One of the glories of Egypt was the famous library at Alexandria. The librarian of that library was Aristophanes of Byzantium. Eumenes of Pergamos cast longing eyes on this Aristophanes, and he tried to lure him from the library at Alexandria to the library at Pergamos. Ptolemy was infuriated that an attempt should be made to seduce so great a scholar and so valuable an asset from his service; so he retaliated by putting Aristophanes in prison, and thereby making it impossible for him to yield to the seductions of Eumenes, and by placing a ban on the export of papyrus to Pergamos. This ban made it necessary for Eumenes to develop the manufacture of parchment from the skins of animals as a substitute for papyrus, and so identified with Pergamos did this new writing material become that it became known as *hē Pergamēnē charta*, the Pergamene sheet. It is an odd and illuminating commentary on the circumstances of the time that the proposed transference of a famous librarian from one library to another provoked such an international crisis!

ii. But it was not only in the realm of literature that Pergamos was internationally famous; it was a famous center of religious worship. John describes it as the place WHERE SATAN'S SEAT IS (Revelation 2.13). And it may well be that it is in the religious fame of Pergamos that we are to look for the meaning of that phrase. Pergamos had two outstanding religious connections.

(*a*) It was the center of the worship of Asklepios, or, as the Romans called him, Aesculapius. Asklepios was the god of healing, and to his temple, the Asklepeion, there came sufferers from all over the ancient world. The temple had its medical wards, its medical schools, its priests and its votaries. R. H. Charles describes Pergamos as 'the Lourdes of the ancient world'. Is there anything in the worship of Asklepios which might account for the fact that John says that Pergamos was the place where Satan's seat was? There are two possibilities.

The characteristic title of Asklepios was *Asklēpios Sōtēr, Asklepios the Savior*. Now *Sōtēr, Savior*, is the word which in the belief of any Christian belongs uniquely and exclusively to Jesus Christ; and it might well be that the Christians felt that the application of this title to a heathen god was indeed a Satanic perversion of the truth.

But there was something even more suggestive than that about the worship of Asklepios. The emblem of Asklepios is the *serpent*. We may still see that emblem on the cap badge of the Royal Army Medical Corps, or on the lapel badge of a Royal Air

Force nursing orderly. The serpent was intimately connected with one of the ways in which cures were effected in the Asklepeion. Sufferers were allowed to spend the night in the darkness of the temple. In the temple there were tame snakes. In the night the sufferer might be touched by one of these tame and harmless snakes as it glided over the ground on which he lay. The touch of the snake was held to be the touch of the god himself, and the touch was held to bring health and healing. To anyone, Jew or Christian, with any knowledge of the Old Testament the serpent is nothing less than the emblem of Satan himself. The serpent was bound to carry the thoughts of any Christian, and especially of any Jewish Christian, back to the old story of man's first sin in the Garden of Eden (Genesis 3). It might well be that the Christians might regard as SATAN'S SEAT the temple of a God whose emblem was the serpent, a temple in which serpents crawled about and were regarded as incarnations of the god himself.

So closely was Asklepios connected with Pergamos that he was sometimes even called the Pergamene god. It may well be that in this we have the origin of the phrase in which Pergamos is called the seat of Satan. But it is doubtful, because there were other cities, in particular Laodicaea, which had the same connection, and the phrase is not applied to them.

ii. Pergamos had always gloried in the fact that she was the last outpost of Greek civilization. Beyond her there lay the wild territories of the uncivilized Celts. Pergamos was therefore proud of the worship of the Greek gods. Behind Pergamos there rose a conical hill which was dotted with the temples and the shrines of the pagan gods; and such a hill might well be known as Satan's seat.

In particular, two of the greatest and the most famous shrines were the shrines of Zeus and Athene, the two greatest of the Greek gods. Half-way up that hill there stood the Temple of

Athene, and in front of it there stood one of the most famous altars in the world, the altar of Zeus. It stood on a ledge which jutted out from the hillside eight hundred feet up. It was ninety feet square and twenty feet high. Round the base of it there was carved the famous frieze which represented the battle of the giants, and which to this day is one of the great masterpieces of sculpture of the world. All day long this altar smoked with the smoke of countless sacrifices to Olympian Zeus. It dominated the city. No one could fail to see it; the eye of anyone in Pergamos was drawn to it. As it stood there on its jutting ledge on the hillside it would look like nothing so much as a great seat or throne. No one could live in Pergamos and not see it.

It may perhaps be that altar which John calls Satan's seat. But again it is not very likely. Even by this time the worship of the Olympian gods was a bankrupt concern. It was hardly worth wasting powder and shot on. The stories of the wars and battles and loves and jealousies and adulteries of the gods and goddesses of Olympus had entirely discredited them. It was not a case of men becoming so depraved that they abandoned their gods; it was a case of the gods becoming so depraved that they were abandoned by men. True, that great altar was there, dominating the landscape for all to see. It might well be described as Satan's seat, but there is an intensity of horror about this phrase which seems to demand more than that.

iii. There was one other direction in which Pergamos enjoyed a religious fame. She was a center of Caesar-worship. Like Smyrna, she was the headquarters of one of these presbyteries into which Caesar-worship had been organized. One of the oddest titles to which any city could lay claim was the title *neokoros*, which means *temple sweeper*. (See also p. 5 above.) When a city erected a temple to a god, its greatest claim to honor was that it became officially the *neokoros*, the temple-sweeper of that god. Of course the sweeping of the temple was the most menial and humble of religious duties. Behind the title there lies an idea which in itself is a lovely idea, that it was a city's greatest privilege to render even the humblest service to the god who had taken up his residence within it. Pergamos was the city which called itself the *neokoros* of the temple where Caesar was worshipped. Pergamos was a city where Caesar-worship was at its most intense, a city dedicated to glorying in the worship of Caesar. That indeed to a Christian would be nothing less than the worship of Satan. In Pergamos it was supremely perilous to be a Christian. There were cities in which danger descended on the Christians on the appointed day when the pinch of incense had to be burned, but where for the most part the Christians were left in peace for the rest of the year. But in Pergamos a Christian was in jeopardy of his life three hundred and sixty-five days in the year. The Christian in Pergamos had taken his life in his hands for the sake of his loyalty to Jesus Christ.

Cromwell before one of his battles addressed his soldiers and told them that they were 'upon an engagement very difficult'. To be a Christian in Pergamos was to be upon such an engagement. There the new-born Church, as yet almost without a history, had to exist against the background of a city proud of its history. There the community of simple Christians had to exist against the background of the academic pride and arrogance of heathenism in all its pagan wisdom. There the simple services of the Church had to exist against the background of the splendor and the magnificence of the worship of the Olympian gods. There the Christians in all their weakness and their helplessness had to preserve their loyalty against the imperial might of Caesar-worship. But even in Pergamos men held fast to the name of Jesus Christ, and refused to deny their faith in Him.

VI
PERGAMOS

Praise and Blame

The letter to the Church at Pergamos begins with the grim statement that the Christians at Pergamos have TO DWELL WHERE SATAN'S SEAT IS. The word which the Authorized Version translates *seat* is *thronos*, which is the same word as the English word *throne*. It means more than merely *seat*; it means *a seat of special authority*. It is, for instance, in Matthew 19.28 the seat of a judge; and in Luke 1.32 it is the throne of a king. Pergamos was therefore not simply the place where Satan existed, but the place where Satan wielded a very special authority. Pergamos was a place where the anti-God forces of the universe were at their most authoritative and most powerful.

It is there that the Church of Pergamos DWELLS. When the New Testament speaks of the Christian dwelling anywhere in this world, it ordinarily uses the Greek word *paroikein* (I Peter 1.1; Hebrews 11.9). *Paroikein* is the word which is characteristically used of a *stranger* and *sojourner*; it is the word which describes a *temporary* residence in contrast with a permanent residence. It is the word which is summed up in the unwritten saying of Jesus: 'The world is a bridge; the wise man will pass over it, but will not build his house upon it.' The word *paroikein* looks on the Christian as a stranger and a pilgrim, who in this world has no permanent home in any city, but

35

whose home is in that city whose maker and builder is God. But the significant thing about this passage is that it is not the word *paroikein* which is used; it is *katoikein*; and *katoikein* is the word that is regularly used for *residence in a permanent and settled place*. What the Risen Christ is saying to the Christians in Pergamos is this: 'You are living in a city where the influence and the power of Satan are rampant – *and you have got to go on living there*. You cannot escape. You cannot pack your baggage and move off to some place where it is easier to be a Christian. In Pergamos you are, and in Pergamos you must stay. Life has set you where Satan's seat is. It is *there* you must live; and it is *there* you must show that you are a Christian.'

The word *katoikein* tells us that it is no part of the Christian duty to run away from a difficult and a dangerous situation. The Christian aim is not escape from a situation, but conquest of a situation.

Kipling has a poem entitled 'Mulholland's Contract'. Mulholland was a cattle-man on a cattle-boat. His place was in the great hold where the cattle were carried. There came a terrific storm at sea; the cattle broke loose; in their terror they were stampeding and trampling everywhere; and it seemed certain that Mulholland would be killed beneath their flailing hooves. So Mulholland made a contract with God.

> An' by the terms of the Contract, as I have read the same,
> If He got me to port alive I would exalt His Name,
> An' praise His Holy Majesty till further orders came.

Miraculously Mulholland was preserved. When he reached shore alive he was prepared to fulfil his part of the contract. His idea was to quit the cattle-boats and to preach religion 'handsome an' out of the wet'. But God's word came to him:

> I never puts on My ministers no more than they can bear.
> So back you go to the cattle-boats, an' preach My Gospel there.

It was Mulholland's duty, not to seek an easier sphere to be a Christian, but to be a Christian exactly where God had set him.

When Jesus had restored to sanity the madman who had dwelt among the tombs of Gerasa, the man besought Jesus to be allowed to come with Him and to remain with Him. Jesus' answer was: 'Go home to thy friends, and tell them how great things the Lord hath done for thee' (Mark 5.1-19). The Christians of Pergamos had to be Christians in Pergamos. No man ever became a Christian by running away.

The Risen Christ goes on to commend the Christians of Pergamos because they were HOLDING FAST TO HIS NAME (verse 13). That is to say, they had never lost their grip on Christ. There was much in Pergamos deliberately calculated to prise them loose from Christ but grimly they had held on.

Further, they had not DENIED HIS FAITH. The word *denied* is in the *aorist* tense. In Greek the aorist points to one particular action done and completed in past time. This phrase then means that in Pergamos there must have been some definite hour of crisis, some definite outburst of persecution, in which the Christians of Pergamos had remained staunch and true.

One martyr of Pergamos is mentioned by name. Of Antipas we know nothing historical, but later legend tells us that he was killed by being roasted to death in a brazen bull. Antipas is called MY FAITHFUL MARTYR. *Martus* is a most interesting and suggestive word. In classical Greek *martus* never means a *martyr* in our sense of the term. It always means a *witness*. A *martus* was one who said: 'This is true, and I know it.' It is not until New Testament times that *martus* ever means *martyr*. There are in fact cases in the New Testament where it is doubtful whether we should translate *martus witness* or *martyr* (Acts 1.8; 22.20; I Timothy 6.13; in Revelation 17.6 it is definitely *martyr*). There is a tremendous truth here. *Martus* means both *witness* and *martyr*; and the very history of the word shows us that *to be a witness is often to be a martyr.* To witness for Christ is often to suffer for Christ. To say of Christ: 'He is true, and I know it' is often the way to trouble and to persecution. To this day the man who is a *witness* for Christ must often be a *martyr* for Christ, not, it is true, in the sense of having to lay down his life for Christ, but in the sense of having to suffer for his Christian principles. It is nothing but the plain truth that, in many cases, if a man took his Christian principles inflexibly with him into his job, he would lose his job. But one thing must be remembered – because Antipas was true *Jesus Christ gave him nothing less than His own title*. In Revelation 1.5 Jesus Christ himself is called THE FAITHFUL MARTUS, and that is the very title that He gave to Antipas. To suffer for Christ is in the end to share the glory of Christ. The crown is always worth the cross.

In verse 14 the tone of the letter changes. The praise stops and rebuke and warning begin. The Balaam reference is to Numbers 31.16. There were those in Pergamos who were trying to teach the people of the Church of Pergamos to sin. They were encouraging them to do two things.

i. They were encouraging them TO EAT THINGS SACRIFICED UNTO IDOLS. Here we are face to face with one of the great social problems of the early Christians. To us it may seem a remote and a recondite matter; to the early Christians it was a burning, and often an agonizing, problem. When a man sacrificed some animal in a heathen temple, ordinarily only a very small part of the animal was burned. Only a token part of the animal, sometimes no more than a few hairs cut from its forehead, was burned in the fire. Of what remained, the priest had a certain share as his perquisite; and the remainder was handed back to the worshipper. The worshipper with his share made a feast for his friends. That feast might be held in his own house, but, even more commonly, it was held in the temple of the god. Invitations to such feasts often read: 'I invite you to dine with me at the temple of our Lord Serapis.' Most family parties were in fact organized in this way. Could a Christian attend such a party? Could he share in a party held in the temple of a heathen god? Could he whose lips had been touched by the holy food of the sacrament take upon these same lips meat that had been offered to the heathen gods? Dare the Christian compromise? Dare he give even this much approval to a religion which was the reverse of all he cherished and believed? The lax and false teachers said yes. They declared it to be quite unnecessary for the Christians to cut themselves off from all social fellowship in this way. They argued the way of conformity, the way of compromise, and, if they had had their way, the Christian Church would have caught the infection of heathenism and would in the end have been swamped in the surrounding sea of paganism. The answer of the Church to all such suggestions of compromise was: 'Stand thou on that side, for on this side am I.'

ii. They were encouraging them TO COMMIT FORNICATION. It has been said that chastity was the one completely new virtue which Christianity introduced into the ancient world. In the ancient world sexual morals were loose; relationships outside marriage were entirely accepted and produced no stigma whatsoever. Demosthenes has laid it down: 'We have courtesans for the sake of pleasure; we have concubines for the sake of daily cohabitation; we have wives for the purpose of having children legitimately, and of having a faithful guardian of our household affairs.' He was not saying anything which was in the least shocking; he was simply laying down the accepted pattern of sexual life. Cicero in his *Pro Caelio* pleads: 'If there is anyone who thinks that young men should be absolutely forbidden the love of courtesans, he is extremely severe. I am not able to deny the principle that he states. But he is at variance, not only with the licence of what our own age allows, but also with the customs and concessions of our ancestors. When indeed was this not done? When did anyone ever find fault with it? When was such permission denied? When was it that that which is now lawful was not lawful?' To Cicero such relationships were an accepted part of the life of a young man. Alexander Severus was one of the reforming Roman emperors, and set his face against vice. Yet the historian Lampridius tells us of him that, when he appointed a man to be governor of a province, he provided him with a horse and a staff of servants, and, if he had no wife, with a concubine, 'because it was not possible that he should exist without one'. Those false teachers who encouraged the Christians of Pergamos to commit fornication were urging them to conform to the accepted standards of the world, and to stop being different. The early Church was in constant danger of being tainted by and relapsing into the standards of the world.

Verse 16 is a verse of justice and mercy combined. The Risen Lord does not say *I will fight against you*: He says: I WILL FIGHT AGAINST THEM. His wrath is not directed against the whole Church, but against those who have taken the wrong way, and who have encouraged others to do so. The greatest anger of Christ is against those who teach others to sin. To sin oneself is forgivable; to teach another to sin is to become liable to the wrath of God.

Verse 17 speaks of the HIDDEN MANNA which he who overcomes will eat. It was the Jewish belief that in the original temple three things had been laid up in the Holy Place before God – Aaron's rod that budded, the stone tables of the Ten Commandments, and a golden pot of the manna which the people had eaten in the wilderness. At the destruction of the temple it was said that the manna had disappeared. One legend said that Jeremiah had hidden it, and would produce it when the Messiah appeared. The manna was to come back when the age of the Messiah dawned. The psalmist called manna the corn of heaven, or angels' food, or the bread of the mighty (Psalm 78.24, 25). Exodus 16.4 calls it bread from heaven. The point is that those who on this earth refused to eat the meat that had been offered to idols would in the world to come eat the bread of God. They might have to give up earthly pleasures, but heavenly joys would be theirs.

The letter ends with the promise of the WHITE STONE with the name that no man knows written upon it. What is the WHITE STONE? There are many possible explanations of this phrase, and each one of them has its own facet of the truth.

i. In ancient times juries voted by casting stones into an urn. A white stone stood for acquittal and a black stone for condemnation. The prisoner was acquitted or condemned according as white or black stones were in the majority. So then this may mean that, if a man is faithful, God will acquit him. His loyalty has stood the test and the trial of God.

ii. In ancient times white stones were used as counters in calculations. This then may mean that, if a man has been faithful, he will be counted, reckoned among the number of the people of God.

iii. In ancient times a white stone was the symbol of a happy day. Pliny talks of a day 'marked by the whitest of white stones.' Especially the white stone was the symbol of a day of victory – as we speak of a 'red-letter day'. This then may mean that the man who is faithful will be reckoned as the victor, and will be welcomed into heaven with the victor's joy.

iv. One of the features of the Roman Empire was free doles of bread, and the free provision of circuses, gladiatorial games and other entertainments. The tickets which entitled to free food and to admission to the entertainments often took the form of a white stone. This then may mean that in the end the faithful will be entertained by God, and will find his joy in Him.

v. But it is probable that the last explanation is the best. In ancient times amulets were very commonly worn. Sometimes they were made of precious metals; but more often they were made of white or of precious stones. The amulet was supposed to keep a person safe; and on the amulet there was mystic writing, and the amulet was held to be doubly effective, if none but the wearer of it knew what was written on it. So the Risen Christ is saying: 'You wear your amulets to keep you safe; you use your superstitious charms to protect you; you who are Christians have no need of that; for the man who has *my name* written on his heart is safe in life and in death.' Even amidst the perils of Pergamos no one could pluck a Christian from the hand of Christ.

VII
THYATIRA

The Threat from the Inside

It is an odd fact that the longest of the letters to the Seven Church as was written to the Church in the smallest and least important of the seven towns. The difficulty of interpreting this letter lies in the fact that we know so little of the background of the life of the Church in Thyatira. The elder Pliny dismisses Thyatira in the almost contemptuous phrase, 'Thyatira and other unimportant communities'. But in order to understand this letter we must gather together such facts about Thyatira as we do possess.

As we have seen, in an age when roads were few and bad, trade tended to travel down the river valleys. Thyatira lay at the mouth of a long valley which connected the valleys of the Hermus and the Caicus rivers. Clearly that was a strategic valley, and through it the railway still runs. In ancient days some of the greatest roads in the world traversed that valley. Through it there ran the great road from Byzantium to Smyrna; and through it there ran the great trade route from Pergamos to Syria.

A town through which such roads ran can never have been a negligible place; and there must always have been some sort of settlement at Thyatira. It was in 290 B.C. that the name of Thyatira emerged in history, and it emerged as the name of a military center. The supreme importance of Thyatira was that it was the gateway to Pergamos, the capital city of Asia. If Thyatira fell, the way to Pergamos lay wide open for any invader. Thyatira was not a natural fortress. There was no hill on which a citadel could be built to command the road and to be defended. In history its function was to fight a delaying action until Pergamos was ready to resist. The result was that Thyatira was one of these sentinel towns, fated to fight and to be captured, to be destroyed and to be rebuilt, because it was on the way to a city and to a prize far greater than itself.

Thyatira was not a center of special religious importance. It had temples of Artemis and Apollo, but they were not specially famous. It was not a special center of Caesar worship. The Church in Thyatira would not be faced by the danger of the splendor of heathen religion, or by the menace of the threat of Caesar worship. The one claim to religious fame which Thyatira possessed was that in it an oriental sibyl called the Sambathē had her shrine, and not a few came to consult that oracle for guidance.

But, if Thyatira was not a great religious center, it certainly was a great commercial center. The roads which passed through its valley brought the trade of half the world to its doors. In particular Thyatira was a great center of the wool trade and of the dyeing industry. It was from Thyatira that Lydia, the seller of purple, came (Acts 16.14). Purple dye was extremely expensive. It came from two sources. It came from the madder root which grew plentifully around Thyatira. And it came from the little shellfish called the *murex*. From the throat of this little animal one drop of purple dye could be extracted. The elder Pliny tells us that this purple dye was so expensive that one pound of it could not be bought for one thousand *denarii*, that is, for about sixty dollars. Lydia must have been a merchant princess, a woman of wealth, dealing in one of the most costly substances in the ancient world. Thyatira, then, was a place of great commercial prosperity and wealth.

But the one outstanding characteristic which distinguished Thyatira from other towns was this – from the inscriptions which have been found in the neighborhood it is clear that Thyatira possessed more trade-guilds than any other town of her size in Asia; and it would seem that the danger which threatened the Church at Thyatira was the direct result of the powerful existence of these trade-guilds. Just how that happened we shall go on to see.

At the center of the situation which threatened Thyatira there was a woman who is given the name of *Jezebel*. The original Jezebel was the daughter of the King of Sidon, and Ahab, King of Israel, had taken her to wife (I Kings 16.31). Her sin was that she had brought with her into Israel her own gods and goddesses. She had brought with her Baal and Astarte and all the rest of them, and had introduced the worship of these strange gods and goddesses into Israel, and had thus defiled the worship of the true God. Clearly, then, this woman of Thyatira, this new Jezebel, was seducing the Christian Church from the worship of the true God. She was teaching them TO COMMIT FORNICATION AND TO EAT THINGS SACRIFICED TO IDOLS. Just as the ancient Jezebel had corrupted the faith of Israel, so this new Jezebel was corrupting the faith of the Christians of Thyatira. Who, then, was this Jezebel? There are three possible answers to that question.

i. In Revelation 2.20 she is called THAT WOMAN JEZEBEL. The Greek word for *woman* and for *wife* is the same word, the word *gunē*. Now certain Greek manuscripts of the Revelation insert after the word *gunaika* (the accusative of the word *gunē*) the word *sou*, which means *yours*. In that case the phrase would mean *Jezebel your wife*. We must add to that the fact that there are certain scholars who think that *the angel* of the Church, to which the letters are addressed, is the *bishop* of the Church.

(*Aggelos* can mean either *angel* or *messenger*, and the *bishop* might well be called God's *messenger* to the Church.) If, then, we put all these facts together we get the interesting possibility that this woman who is called Jezebel was the wife of the bishop of the Church, and that she was a fertile source of trouble, and was, in fact, undoing all the good work her husband did. It is an interesting theory, but the manuscript evidence for the insertion of the word *sou* is not good enough to allow us to accept it beyond doubt.

ii. It has been suggested that this woman who is called Jezebel is to be identified with the famous local oracle called the *Sambathē*. It is just possible that the *Sambathē* may have been a Jewess. Most Jews remained stubbornly loyal to their faith; but even amongst the Jews there were a few renegades; and the odd thing is that these ancient Jewish renegades not infrequently became sooth-sayers, fortune-tellers, and astrologers. In a superstitious world it was a line of activity which was extremely profitable financially and which gave them a very commanding influence over those who sought their help. It has therefore been suggested that the *Sambathē* was a renegade Jewess, who had flung all her very considerable influence into an attempt to destroy the Christian worship and the Christian ethic. That again is an interesting theory; but it hardly fits the facts, because the whole tone of the letter proves that the peril which was threatening the Christians of Thyatira came, not from *outside*, but from *inside* the Church.

iii. So we come to the third theory, and it is the theory which best fits the facts. We have already seen that the most notable fact about Thyatira was the quite unusual number of trade-guilds which flourished within it. This must have presented the Christians of Thyatira with a very real problem. No merchant or trader could hope to prosper and to make money unless he was a member of his trade-guild. If a trader refused to join his trade-guild, he would be in much the same position as a working-man would be today, if he refused to join his trade union. Such a man has little hope of getting a job, and such a trader would have little hope of gaining any trade. But, we may well ask, why should a Christian of Thyatira not join just such a trade-guild?

The social activities of these trade-guilds were intimately bound up with the worship of the heathen gods. These trade-guilds had common meals together. The meal would begin and end with a cup of wine poured out as a libation and an offering to the gods. It was, in fact, the heathen grace before and after meat. Could a Christian join in a ceremony like that? Still further, such a meal would almost certainly follow a sacrifice. The token part of the animal would be offered on the altar. The meat of it would be given to the worshipper to make a feast for the members of his trade-guild. Could a Christian sit and eat *meat which had been offered to idols*? Could he partake of a meal where the meat had already been offered to Apollo or Artemis or to Tyrimnus, the local God? Still further, these trade-guild feasts not infrequently degenerated into carousals, where drunkenness and immorality were the order of the day. Could a Christian participate in a feast where drunkenness and fornication were the accepted things?

There is obviously a very real problem here. If in Thyatira the Christian merchant or trader or craftsman was a member of his trade-guild, and participated in its ceremonies, he would protect his business interests and ensure his material prosperity; if he refused to become a member of such a guild and refused to participate in its ceremonies, he was very definitely committing commercial suicide and would very soon be faced with poverty, and even bankruptcy.

The Church never had any doubt as to what the Christian must do. T. R. Glover points out how Tertullian's tract *On*

Idolatry deals with this very question. There he deals with Christians who earn their living by making idols – statuaries, painters, gilders and the like; and when the plea is suggested that they *must* live and have no other way of living, he indignantly retorts that they should have thought this out before. *Vivere ergo habes*? *Must* you live? he asks (Tertullian, *De Idol.*, 5). Elsewhere he says: 'There are no *musts* where faith is concerned' (*De Cor. Mil.*, 11). The Church was certain that the Christian must divorce himself entirely from these things, that he must by deliberate decision keep his garments unspotted from the world. But it was asking a great deal; and all the likelihood is that this woman, who is called Jezebel, argued and insisted that Christians should become members of the trade-guilds, that they should attend the heathen functions, that they should compromise with the heathen world and with heathen worship, in order to protect their business interests.

The suggestion has been made that this Jezebel was in fact none other than Lydia, the merchant princess! It has been suggested that, when Lydia returned to Thyatira, she found her Christianity clashing with her business interests, and urged the Church to the way of compromise and accommodation. That is no doubt a slander on Lydia, but it is true that Lydia and every other Christian in Thyatira would have to choose between business prosperity and loyalty to Jesus Christ. The problem which faced every Christian in Thyatira was whether they were to make money or to be Christians. This woman, who is called Jezebel, must have been a woman of strong personality, of great ambition, and of powerful persuasive influence, who argued that the Christian ought to compromise with the world. If her arguments had succeeded, it would have been the end of the Christian Church. Beyond a doubt compromise would have meant absorption in heathenism; the continued existence of the

Church depended on the continued determination of the Church to be different from the world.

This is a situation which is by no means dead today. It is, in fact, a situation which is very much alive. When membership of a trade union, a trade association, a business society demands conduct and action and practice which are not Christian, what is a Christian to do? It is very doubtful if, in a world of restrictive practices, limitation of effort, the search for the maximum pay for the minimum activity, a Christian doctrine of work can be carried out at all. Is trade to come first, or is Christ to come first? Are the demands of membership of the trade association to come first, or are the demands of membership of the Church to come first? Are the principles of worldly business to come first, or are the principles of Christ to come first? The situation in Thyatira is curiously modern. There are thousands of men and women today who are either facing or evading the very same choice as confronted the Christians of Thyatira eighteen hundred years ago.

And the interesting thing about the situation at Thyatira is that the threat to the Church did not come from *outside* the Church. It was not the threat of persecution; it did not come from the panoply of heathen worship; it did not come from the state insistence on Caesar worship. It came from *inside* the Church; it came from those within the Church who proposed to face the world with the most dangerous of all doctrines, a doctrine of compromise. *So true today*

VIII
THYATIRA

The Temptation to Compromise

REVELATION 2.18-29

In verse 19 there is another example of the epexegetic *and* which we have already met in the letter to Ephesus in Revelation 2.2. The epexegetic *and* does not merely add something to that which has gone before; it introduces something which further explains and defines that which has gone before. So then the translation of verse 19 should run: 'I KNOW YOUR WORKS – I MEAN YOUR CHARITY, AND YOUR SERVICE, YOUR FAITH AND YOUR LOVE, AND ALL THAT YOU DO.'

It is to be noted how these great words go in pairs. CHARITY issues in SERVICE; FAITH issues in ENDURANCE. It is as if the Risen Lord was saying: 'If you claim to have Christian love in your heart, you can only prove it by showing that you have Christian service in your life. If you claim to have Christian faith in your soul, you can only prove it by living a life which triumphantly overcomes the world.' As someone has put it: 'The possession of a virtue can only be proved and guaranteed by a life that fits it.'

But there is something very interesting about this verse. The letter to the Church at Thyatira is to be a letter of warning and of criticism, and yet it begins with a verse of undiluted praise. Here is something which every preacher and teacher must learn. Real criticism must always *encourage* and never *discourage*.

50

When we have reason to rebuke or to criticize anyone, we must make it clear that we are doing so, not because we *dislike* him, but because we *like* him; not because we *hate* him, but because we *love* him; not because we think that he is *useless*, but because we think that he has it in him to be *useful*; not because we wish to *hurt* him, but because we wish to *help* him. That is why criticism will often be most effective when it begins with praise. It is wise to point out that which is good, before we begin to seek to eradicate that which is evil.

Verse 20 presents us with the picture of a woman who is obviously a person of very considerable importance and influence in the Church, a woman who claims to be a PROPHETESS. We are very apt to misunderstand the place of women in the early Church. We are apt to think of such sayings of Paul as: 'Let women be silent in the churches, for it is not fitting for them to speak' (I Corinthians 14.34); or, 'I do not allow a woman to teach' (I Timothy 2.12). But we must remember that women who were prophetesses were by no means unknown. Philip the evangelist had four virgin daughters who were prophetesses (Acts 21.9). Luke tells us of Anna the prophetess (Luke 2.36). The Old Testament tells us of Miriam and Huldah and Deborah. When we are trying to find guidance as to the place of women in the early Church, we must remember that when Paul spoke about women as he did in the letters to the Corinthians, he was writing to the most licentious city in the ancient world, and that in such a place modesty had to be observed and more than observed; and that it is quite unfair to wrest a local ruling from the circumstances in which it was given, and to make it a universal principle. And we would do well to remember that it is the full and final teaching of this same Paul that in Christ there is neither Jew nor Greek, bond nor free, male nor female (Galatians 3.28; Colossians 3.11). There is ample evidence that women did in fact have a noble share in the work of the early Church.

In Thyatira this Jezebel, this evil woman, this false prophetess, taught those who would listen to her TO COMMIT FORNICATION AND TO EAT THINGS OFFERED TO IDOLS. When the Gentiles were allowed into the Church on equal terms with the Jews, these were two of the very things which they were forbidden to do by the decree of the Council of Jerusalem (Acts 15.20). As we saw, this woman was most likely urging upon the Christians of Thyatira that there was no harm in attending the meetings of the heathen trade-guilds. She was urging them to court that very infection from which the Church had ordered them to keep themselves free.

In verse 22 the threat is: I WILL CAST HER INTO A BED. There are two possible meanings here. The word translated *bed* is *klinē*. *Klinē* is also the word for a *banqueting-couch*, and, if that meaning be taken, the meaning is: 'I will strike her down as she sits at her forbidden feasts.' If *klinē* is taken to mean a *bed*, the meaning will be: 'If she goes on as she is doing, she will be cast upon a bed of sickness, and disaster will come upon her.' The warning is made even more serious by the words of verse 21, which say that this woman has already been warned, and has been given SPACE TO REPENT. Nothing but disaster can come to the person who is impervious to the repeated warnings of God.

Verses 21-23 speak of FORNICATION and ADULTERY and the CHILDREN of this evil woman. These phrases and expressions can be taken in two ways. They can be taken quite *literally*; they can be taken to mean that this woman has taught and practised a loose and shameful sexual immorality, and that she and her paramours and the offspring of her wicked unions are doomed to disaster.

More likely these expressions are to be taken *figuratively*. One of the favorite pictures of the Old Testament is that of Israel as *the bride of God*. When Israel was unfaithful and untrue to God, it was as if she broke the marriage vow which existed between herself and God. So the people are said to go 'awhoring after the gods of the land' (I Chronicles 5.25). Hosea accuses the nation that the people have gone 'awhoring from thy God' (Hosea 9.1). The metaphor of adultery is the vivid picture of spiritual infidelity to God. Most likely that is the picture here. The *fornication* of Jezebel is her infidelity to God. Those who commit *adultery* with her (the meaning is, those who commit adultery *in company with her*, those who follow her bad example and leading) are those who, as we say, *flirt* with the pernicious doctrines which she teaches. Her *children* are those who have accepted her teaching, and who have taken her forbidden way. The vow to God and the marriage vow are alike in that they must not be broken.

In verse 23 the Risen Lord says that He SEARCHES THE REINS AND THE HEARTS. The *reins* (*nephroi*) are the *kidneys*. In Hebrew psychology the *kidneys* are the seat of the *emotions*. The *heart* (*kardia*) is the seat of the *thoughts*. In other words, as the Hebrews saw it, the *kidneys*, the *reins*, are the *emotional* center of a man's being, and *heart* is the *intellectual* center of man's being. So when the Risen Lord says that He will search the *reins* and the *heart*, it means, to put it in modern language, that there is not a *feeling* and that there is not a *thought* of our inmost beings which is not open to His gaze; our *emotional* life and our *intellectual* life are both laid bare to His scrutiny. There is nothing that we feel or will that He does not know. It is told that once an architect offered to construct a house for Plato in such a way that no one could see into any room of it. Plato's answer was: 'I will give you twice as much, if you build a house for me into every room of which everyone can see.' Happy is the man who feels that his inmost desires and thoughts can bear the scrutiny of both men and God. Only Christ can so cleanse us that we can bear the gaze of His own eyes.

Verse 24 describes those who have gone wrong in the Church

at Thyatira as THOSE WHO HAVE KNOWN THE DEEP THINGS OF SATAN. This may refer to either of two things. i. In the early Church there were certain men called *Gnostics*. These *Gnostics* declared that to be real Christians men must know far more than the simple truths of the gospel, that a special secret knowledge was needed, and they claimed to be able to supply it. They tried to make Christianity into an elaborate philosophy and theosophy. They claimed to be able to provide men with the really *deep things of God*. It is as if the Risen Christ was saying: 'These men who claim that the gospel needs to be developed and filled out with their ideas and their speculative intellectualism are not really teaching you the deep things of God; they are in fact teaching you the DEEP THINGS OF SATAN.' ii. In the early Church there were certain men who said that the really wise and mature Christian must know life at its worst as well as at its best, that he must deliberately experience the lowest as well as the highest. They therefore thought that it was right and necessary to commit the grossest and the most depraved sins, in order to experience what they were like. In effect, they were teaching that a man must sow his wild oats, before he could really appreciate what virtue was. Such teaching was to encourage men to know THE DEEP THINGS OF SATAN, and not the deep things of God.

Verse 26 speaks of the man who OVERCOMES AND KEEPS MY WORKS UNTO THE END. There are two essential things in Christianity. One is a *victory*, and the other is a *long fidelity*. The Christian life does not consist in one victory over sin; it consists in a life-long fidelity which defies every assault of sin. The Christian life is not a *battle*; it is a *campaign*.

Verses 26 and 27 are a quotation from Psalm 2.9. That Psalm was always held to be a forecast and a picture of the triumphant work of God's conquering Messiah. It is an amazing act of faith that the little Christian Church, which was under attack by the vast Roman Empire, should take that promise and appropriate it to itself. From every human point of view the only thing which could possibly await the Church was total destruction and annihilation; but from the divine point of view the thing which awaits the Church is total triumph. It was the conviction of the early Church that the menacing might of Rome was as nothing compared with the gracious power of God.

Verse 28 has the lovely promise of the MORNING STAR. That may mean one of two things. i. It may be *a promise of resurrection*. As the morning star rises over the darkness of the night, so the Christian will rise over the darkness of death. The Christian life, even at its hardest and its darkest, looks, not to the sunset, but to the dawn. ii. It may be *a promise of Christ Himself*. In Revelation 22.16 the Risen Christ says: 'I am the bright and morning star.' The man who is faithful unto death will receive the greatest prize of all – he will receive no other and no less than Jesus Christ Himself.

IX
SARDIS

The Peace of Death

Thirty miles south-east of Thyatira lay Sardis, one of the oldest and most storied cities in Asia Minor. Its position made it one of the world's great trading centers, and wealth poured in upon it. Sardis commanded the Hermus valley, and the whole trade of that rich valley centered upon it. But Sardis' greatest advantage was that it was the center of a knot of five different roads. One road led north-west to Thyatira and then on to Pergamos; another ran west to Smyrna, fifty-four miles away; another ran east and out to Phrygia; another ran south-east to Philadelphia, and then on to the towns of the Maeander valley; another led south-west to Ephesus, sixty-three miles away, and linked Sardis with the valley of the Cayster. A city centered like that could not be otherwise than a magnet to draw trade and wealth to itself.

Sardis had been the ancient capital of the kingdom of Lydia, and away back in 560 B.C. Croesus, whose name has become a proverb for wealth, was its king. It is of interest to note that the first coinage ever to be minted in Asia Minor was minted in Sardis in the days of Croesus. These roughly formed electrum staters were the beginning of money in the modern sense of the term. Sardis was the place where modern money was born.

We have only to read this letter to see that the keyword for it is the word WATCH! (Revelation 3.2-3). There was a reason for that. Sardis was captured by the Persian king Cyrus in the most memorable way. The story is told in the most vivid way by the

56

Greek historian Herodotus (Herodotus 1.84). From her position Sardis was regarded as well nigh impregnable. Behind her there rose Mount Tmolus; from that mountain there went out a narrow ridge of rock like a pier, and on that ridge the citadel of Sardis was built. It was a position which seemed to defy assault. Cyrus was besieging Sardis, and he wished to capture it with all speed, for he could not advance until Sardis was taken. He sent a message to his troops that there would be a special reward for any man who worked out a method whereby this unscalable cliff could be scaled and this untakable fortress taken. In his army there was a Mardian soldier called Hyeroeades. Hyeroeades gazed at the cliffs, seeking to figure out a way by which they might be stormed. He saw a Lydian soldier on the battlements, and, as he watched, the Lydian accidentally dropped his helmet over the battlements, down the cliff. Hyeroeades saw this Lydian mount the battlements, pick his way down the cliffs, recover his helmet, and climb back. Hyeroaedes carefully marked in his memory the way the Lydian soldier had taken. That night he led a picked band of troops up the cliffs by that way, and when they reached the top, they found the battlements completely unguarded. The garrison never dreamed that anyone could find a way up the cliffs. They felt themselves completely safe. So Hyeroeades and his comrades entered in unopposed, and Sardis was taken. The curious thing is that the very same thing happened in the campaigns of Antiochus two hundred years later. The Church at Sardis would hear the word *Watch!* with a memory of how necessary history had proved watchfulness to be. They would know all too well how easily the man who is too secure can find himself in disaster.

In the later days Sardis was a free and self-governing Greek city. For a time it passed from history; not that it did not prosper, but simply that it was not involved in any events which left their record in history. In Roman times Sardis emerged again, still great and still prosperous. The Romans made it an assize town, where justice for the district was dispensed, and it must have been well acquainted with the pomp and panoply of the coming of the Roman governors and their entourage.

Then in A.D. 17 misfortune befell Sardis. It was devastated by an earthquake. But even then its good fortune did not fail it. Tiberius, the reigning Roman Emperor, remitted all taxation for a period of five years, and contributed no less than 10,000,000 sesterces (about $185,000) to aid the city in the task of rebuilding its shattered splendors. In A.D. 26 Strabo, the geographer, could describe it as a *great city*, for it had risen from the ruins and regained its former grandeur. It is little wonder that it was soon competing with Smyrna for the right to build a temple to the godhead of Caesar, a competition which it lost and which Smyrna won.

Let us now assemble the outstanding characteristics of the city of Sardis.

i. Sardis was a great commercial center and extremely wealthy. Through it there ran the gold-bearing river called the Pactolus. Herodotus (5.101) tells us: 'The stream which comes down from Mount Tmolus and which brings Sardis a quantity of gold dust, runs directly through the market place of the city.' It seemed that even nature herself was conspiring to bring wealth to Sardis

ii. Sardis was a great center of the woolen industry. Out in Phrygia the great sheep-masters grazed their flocks, and Sardis was their market. Sardis was indeed the greatest distributing center of the woolen trade. Like Thyatira, it was also a center of the trade in costly dyes. It may be that the reference in Revelation 3.4 to those WHO HAVE NOT DEFILED THEIR GARMENTS is a reference to the woolen trade at Sardis, as if the Risen Christ was saying to it that it might be rich in material garments but the garments of its soul were soiled and shoddy things.

iii. Sardis was not a center of Caesar worship, although it would have liked to have been. It was a center of the worship of Cybele. That worship was a wild, frenzied, hysterical affair, but it was not dangerous to the Christians as Caesar worship would have been.

iv. But the great characteristic of Sardis was that, even on pagan lips, Sardis was a name of contempt. Its people were notoriously loose-living, notoriously pleasure- and luxury-loving. Sardis was a city of the decadence. In the old days it had been a frontier town on the borders of Phrygia, but now it was a by-word for slack and effeminate living. Every day Sardis grew wealthier, but the more wealthy it grew, the more it lost all claim to greatness. Herodotus wrote contemptuously of it and of its people: 'The tender-footed Lydians, who can only play on the cithara, strike the guitar, and sell by retail.' To put it in our modern idiom, Sardis had become a city of amateur dance-band musicians and shopkeepers. Even the heathen would have known what the Risen Christ meant, when He said that Sardis had a name that it was living, but was dead.

The strange fate of Sardis was that life had been too easy for it. It had grown flabby and had sunk into an easy and voluptuous decadence. And the fate of the Church at Sardis was the same. When we read this letter, we see that the Church at Sardis was not threatened by any of the dangers or perils which menaced the other Churches. There was no threat from Caesar worship and from persecution; there was no threat from the malignant slanders of the Jews; there was not even any threat of internal heresy from within the Church. The Church of Sardis was completely untroubled from without and from within. The Church of Sardis was at peace – but it was the peace of the dead.

There are two kinds of peace. There is the peace of conquest and achievement, the peace which comes after a great effort into which a man has put everything that he is and has. And there is the peace of the man who has ceased to care, the peace of the man who has sunk into a comfortable lethargy, the peace of the man whose dreams are dead, and whose mind is asleep, the peace of evasion and escape. Sir William Watson, in his poem 'Wordsworth's Grave', describes the true peace:

> What hadst thou that could make so large amends
>   For all thou hadst not, and thy peers possessed,
> Motion and fire, swift means to radiant ends? -
>   Thou hadst for weary feet, the gift of rest.
>
> From Shelley's dazzling glow or thunderous haze,
>   From Byron's tempest anger, tempest mirth,
> Men turned to thee and found – not blast and blaze,
>   Tumult of tottering heavens, but peace on earth.
>
> Not peace that grows by Lethe, scentless flower,
>   There in white languors to decline and cease;
> But peace whose names are also rapture, power,
>   Clear sight and love; for these are parts of peace.

In any Church there is nothing to be so much desired as peace; but in any Church there is nothing to be so much feared as the peace which is the peace of death, the peace of languorous lethargy, the peace which had descended on Sardis and its Church.

X
SARDIS

The Church of the Living Death

REVELATION 3.1-6

In verse 1 the Risen Christ begins with the grim statement that the Church at Sardis had A NAME THAT IT WAS ALIVE BUT THAT IN FACT IT WAS DEAD. In material things the Church at Sardis might have a certain prosperity, but in everything that mattered it was dead. Materially it was alive; spiritually it was dead. When is it that a Church is in danger of death?

i. A Church is in danger of death when it begins to worship its own past, when it lives on its memories instead of finding a challenge in its hopes, when it is more taken up with its traditions than its ideals.

ii. A Church is in danger of death when it is more concerned with forms than with life. There are Churches which are more concerned with correct ritual than they are with living vitality. There are, for instance, Churches where any kind of talk to children is taboo, because it would disturb the liturgical perfection of the service. When a Church becomes more concerned with how things are done than with the ultimate object of doing them at all, it is on the way to death.

iii. A Church is in danger of death when it loves systems more than it loves Jesus Christ. There are Churches where an infringement of the constitution is the most deadly of sins, and where the book of practice and procedure is second only – if it is second – in authority to the Bible. When the Church becomes the battle-ground of the congregational ecclesiastical lawyer, it is on the way to death.

iv. A Church is in danger of death when it is more concerned with material than with spiritual things. The danger that any Church runs is that it should become a club. Every church activity is necessary, but only as it subserves the primary activity of bringing men and women face to face with Jesus Christ.

In verse 2 there is the command TO BE WATCHFUL. We have already seen that the history of Sardis was itself an illustration of that necessity. There are two points at which every man must be upon the watch.

i. We must be watchful *at our weak point*. Every man has his weak point. In the old days the stone-breaker used to be seen breaking the stones which were to be used in the making of roads. He sat there with his hammer; but he never struck the stone hard. He simply tapped and tapped at it, until the hammer hit the weak spot in the stone, and then the stone disintegrated. Temptation works in exactly the same way. Bradley in his *Shakespearean Tragedy* works out the theory that every one of the main figures in Shakespeare's great tragedies were truly great men, who had one fatal weakness, and that fatal flaw was the ruin of themselves and of those who loved them. With Macbeth it was ambition; with Othello it was jealousy; with Hamlet it was indecision; but in every case the flaw was fatal. The Greeks laid it down that the first law of life must be: 'Know thyself.' That is good advice. There may be in us a habit, a quirk of character, a peculiarity of temperament, a weakness. We must be honest enough to recognize it, and at that point to be upon our guard.

ii. We must be watchful *at our strongest point*. That is

precisely what Sardis had failed to be when its citadel was taken. Over and over again strongholds have been captured because their defenders thought them too strong to be attacked. If ever we say of anything. 'That is one thing at least which I would never do', that is the very thing against which we ought to be on our guard. Lord Fisher, the great sailor, had a favorite saying: 'Life is strewn with orange peel.' The great saying runs: 'Eternal vigilance is the price of liberty.' Watchfulness is an absolute necessity of life, for we never know when we may slip.

In verse 2 the Risen Christ goes on to say: I HAVE NOT FOUND THY WORKS PERFECT BEFORE GOD. Here we are face to face with a great truth – not only are we looking for something from Jesus Christ; *Jesus Christ is looking for something from us.* In the Church of Sardis He did not find that for which He was looking. There are two things for which Jesus Christ is specially looking.

i. He is looking for our *loyalty*. Every leader needs followers who are loyal. Field-Marshal Montgomery used to say in the days of the war: 'One man can lose me a battle.' One man can let Christ down.

ii. He is looking for our *help*. We speak much of the power of Jesus Christ, but, startling as it may seem, there is a sense in which we can speak of the *helplessness* of Jesus Christ. It is the simple truth that, if Jesus wishes something done, He has to get a man to do it for Him. If He wants a child taught, He has to get a man or a woman to teach that child, or that child will never be taught. If He wants a sufferer healed, He has to get a doctor, a physician, a surgeon, a man of prayer to carry out that healing, or at least to be the channel of the healing. There is a passage in *My lady of the Chimney Corner*: 'God takes a han' wherever He can find it, an' jist dizz what He likes wi' it. Sometimes He takes a Bishop's hand, an' lays it on a child's head in benediction; then He takes the han' of a docther t' relieve pain, th' han' of a mother t' guide her chile, an' sometimes He takes the han' of an auld craither like me t' give a bit of comfort to a neighbor. But they're all han's touch't by His Spirit, an' His Spirit is everywhere lukin' for han's to use.' There is a selfish Christianity which is for ever looking for things from Jesus, and which forgets to ask: 'What is Jesus looking for from me?'

In verse 3 there is suggestiveness in the Greek tenses which are used. REMEMBER is a present imperative; and the present imperative expresses continuous action. It means: 'Go on remembering; don't ever let yourself forget.' Faith is something which we have *received.* RECEIVED is the perfect tense, and means something which *we have received and of which we have possession.* The Christian faith is a trust which has been given to us. Over and over again in the Pastoral Epistles we get the idea of the Christian faith as a deposit (*parathēkē*). The word is the same word as is used to describe that which is deposited with a banker for safe-keeping. The Christian faith is something with which we have been entrusted, and which we must hand on intact and unharmed. The Christian faith is something we have HEARD. It comes to us through the words and teachings of others. They are the link between us and Christ, and we in turn must be the link between Christ and those who are to come. We are urged to REPENT. In this case the imperative is the aorist imperative which implies one definite action completed in past time. It points to one definite moment when we turned our backs upon sin and our faces to Christ. There must be some time when, like the man with the very stout countenance in the *Pilgrim's Progress*, we say: 'Set down my name, sir.' That moment of decision need not be a moment of public decision, but there must be some moment in life when we definitely decide for Christ. We are urged to HOLD FAST. In this case it is the present imperative, denoting continuous action. After the moment of decision, there must come the life-time of constant loyalty. When William Carey was an old man, he was talking to his nephew about the possibility that some day someone might write his life. He said: 'If he gives me credit for being a plodder, he will describe me justly. Anything beyond this will be too much. I can plod. I can persevere in any definite pursuit. To this I owe everything.' In the Christian life there are two essentials, the ability to make the clear-cut decision at the crucial moment, and the ability to plod on on the Christian way for a whole life-time.

Verse 4 speaks about those WHO HAVE NOT DEFILED THEIR GARMENTS. That would be readily understood by those who came from Greek religion, because in Greek religion it was sacrilege to approach the gods in garments that were soiled and stained. For the Greeks that was merely an outward thing; for us it is the inner purity of the heart which will alone enable us to see God.

In verse 5 there is the promise of THE WHITE RAIMENT. In ancient times *white robes* stood for three things. i. They stood for *purity*. Only the pure in heart shall see God. It is with the purity of His own merits that Christ will clothe us. ii. They stood for *festivity*. The white robe was the robe of feasting. The joy of heaven will be a festal joy. Unless our Christianity brings us joy, it brings us nothing. iii. They stood for *victory*. The white robe was the victor's robe. It is ours to share in the victory of Christ.

Verse 5 also speaks of THE BOOK OF LIFE. This phrase occurs in the Old Testament in Exodus 32.32; Psalm 69.28; Malachi 3.16; Daniel 12.1; Psalm 139.16. In ancient times cities kept a register of their citizens, and when a man died his name was removed from the register. The Risen Christ is saying that, if we wish to remain on the roll of the citizens of God, we must keep our faith flamingly alive.

The state of the Church at Sardis was serious, but it was not beyond hope; the words of the Risen Christ are a condemnation, but they are also a summons and a challenge to awake, while yet there is time.

> He speaks, and, listening to His voice
> New life the dead receive.

While life remains, there is still time for faith to be awakened, and for the dead heart to come alive.

XI
PHILADELPHIA

The Gateway of a Great Opportunity

Twenty-eight miles south-east of Sardis lay the city of Philadelphia. As cities went, it was not very ancient, for it had been founded by Attalus the Second in 140 B.C. Attalus was called *Philadelphos*, and it was after him that Philadelphia had been named. Although Philadelphia as a city was not very ancient, from the earliest times there had always been some kind of settlement on the site where it stood. It was one of the most strategic sites in the world. Philadelphia stood at the place where the borders of three countries – Mysia, Lydia and Phrygia – met. It was characteristically a border town.

Because of its position Philadelphia was the gateway to the East. Herodotus (7.31) tells us a pleasant story about the place where Philadelphia was one day to stand. When Xerxes the Persian king was on his way to invade Europe, he found shelter there under the shade of a great plane tree. He so admired the tree and felt such gratitude to it that he decked it out with costly gifts, and left a personal bodyguard to care for it and to look after it. Philadelphia commanded one of the greatest highways in the world, the highway which led from Europe to the East. Philadelphia was the gateway from one continent to another.

It was for that very reason that Attalus had built Philadelphia. Philadelphia had been built with the deliberate intention that it might become a missionary city. Beyond Philadelphia lay the wilds of Phrygia and the barbarous tribes; and it was intended that the function of Philadelphia should be to spread the Greek language, the Greek way of life, the Greek civilization throughout the regions beyond. Philadelphia was intended to be the missionary of Hellenism to the wilds of Phrygia. It had been the function of Sardis to do the same for Lydia, and Sardis had performed her function so effectively that the Lydians had almost forgotten their own native language, and had become completely Hellenized. But Philadelphia had not been so successful; the Phrygians were much more impervious to Greek ways than the Lydians had been. They had remained stubbornly Phrygian, and had refused to become Hellenized. But the aim of Attalus for Philadelphia had been that it should be a missionary to the barbarians of all things Greek.

It was of that that the Risen Christ was thinking when He said: BEHOLD, I HAVE SET BEFORE THEE AN OPEN DOOR (Revelation 3.8). The door was the door of opportunity. In the old days it had been the function of Philadelphia to be the missionary of Hellenism to the wide, wild lands which stretched beyond her. Now in the fulness of time the door of opportunity was wide open again; but this time the opportunity was to bring to the lands beyond, not the gospel of Hellenism, but the gospel of Christ. Philadelphia was the city before whom there opened the door to virgin territory to be won for Christ. Philadelphia was the city for whom the door of opportunity was swinging on its hinges.

Philadelphia had another characteristic which lights up the letter written to it. It lay on the edge of a great plain called *The Katakekaumenē*, which means *The Burnt Land*. It lay on the edge of a great volcanic area. In one way this brought Philadelphia tremendous prosperity, for that great plain was one of the most fertile areas in the world. It was a great grape-growing area, and Philadelphia was world-famous for her vintages and her wines. Further, it was an area rich in hot springs, and Philadelphia was, and still is, a center to which the infirm came to bathe in the medicinal waters. The products of Philadelphia's prosperity went out to the ends of the earth; and into it there came people from many a land in the search for health and healing.

But the very fact which brought prosperity to Philadelphia also brought danger. Because it was on the edge of this volcanic area, Philadelphia was very subject to earthquakes. In the earthquake of A.D. 17 Philadelphia was also devastated and laid waste; but Tiberius the Roman Emperor extended to it the same generosity as he had extended to Sardis; he remitted its taxes and gave it a very large contribution towards the task of rebuilding the shattered city. In gratitude for what Tiberius had done Philadelphia changed its name to *Neocaesarea*, The New Town of Caesar. The promise of the Risen Christ to His faithful servant is: I WILL WRITE MY NEW NAME UPON HIM (Revelation 3.12). Philadelphia knew all about a change of name because of gratitude for benefits conferred. It is true that the new name Neocaesarea did not last, and Philadelphia reverted to its old name. But once, in gratitude for what Tiberius had done, the new name of Neocaesarea had been written on Philadelphia; and now in gratitude for still greater things the new name of Jesus Christ was written upon it.

Because of their situation the citizens of Philadelphia lived an unsettled and a tremulous life. Whenever the earthquake tremors came, and they came often, the people of Philadelphia fled from the city out into the open country, to escape the falling masonry and the flying stones which accompanied a severe earthquake shock. Then, when the earth was quiet again, they returned. In their fear the people of Philadelphia were always going out and coming in; they were always fleeing from the city and then returning to it. This frightened rhythm of flight and return had become part of their lives. The promise of the Risen

Christ to His faithful servant is: HE SHALL GO NO MORE OUT (Revelation 3.12). It is the promise of safety. It is as if the Risen Christ said to the people of Philadelphia: 'I can rid you of your fears and of your terrors; I can rid you of your nervous uncertainties; I can give you a safety that will keep you safe in life and in death.' It was not protection from death that the Risen Christ offered; it was deliverance from the fear of death. The fear of the earthquake had sent them scurrying for safety again and again. All our days the fear of life and the fear of death make us seek some kind of security which will keep us safe in all the chances and the changes of this uncertain existence. It is just that safety that Jesus Christ offers to those who give their lives to Him. It is the safety of the man who knows that nothing in life or death can separate him from the love of God.

Philadelphia had still another custom which finds its echo in the letter written to it. Philadelphia was a famous center of heathen worship. Not unnaturally her principal god was Dionysius, the god of wine. Since the grape gave Philadelphia so much of her prosperity, it was natural that it should worship the god of the grape. But Philadelphia had so many gods and so many temples that sometimes men called her 'little Athens'. To walk through her temple-scattered streets was to be reminded of Athens, the center of the worship of the Olympian gods.

Philadelphia had a lovely custom which concerned these temples. When a man had served the state well, when he had left behind him a noble record as a magistrate or as a public benefactor or as a priest, the memorial which the city gave to him was to erect a pillar in one of the temples with his name inscribed upon it. Philadelphia honored its illustrious sons by putting their names on the pillars of its temples, so that all who came to worship might see and remember. So the Risen Christ promises to the man who overcomes: I WILL MAKE HIM A PILLAR IN THE TEMPLE OF MY GOD (Revelation 3.12). Not in any heathen temple, but in the very house and family of God, will the name of the man who is faithful be inscribed.

All through this letter to Philadelphia we see how the message of the Risen Christ came to the people of Philadelphia in language and in pictures that they could understand. He took its history, He took the things that happened in everyday life, He took the civic practices which all men knew, and out of these earthly things He formed the heavenly message. The letter to Philadelphia is a unique example of how to use *the here and now* to get to *the there and then*.

The letter to Philadelphia is a letter of undiluted praise. In later days, when Islam swept across Asia Minor, for many a year Philadelphia stood as the last bastion of Christianity. When it fell, it did not fall through weakness or lack of courage; it fell because in the end it was actually betrayed by its fellow-Christians of Byzantium, who were jealous of its honor. To this day Philadelphia is a Christian town with a Christian bishop. Philadelphia is the town which kept the faith.

XII
PHILADELPHIA

The Church which kept the Faith

REVELATION 3.7-13

This letter begins in verse 7 with two great descriptions of the Risen Lord.

First, He is called HE THAT IS TRUE. In Greek there are two words which are both translated *true*. The first is the word *alēthēs*, which is the word which describes a statement that is *true*, and not false. The second is the word *alēthinos*, which means *true* in the sense of *real* or *genuine*, as opposed to illusory and spurious. It is *alēthinos* which is used here. Jesus is the one person who is *real* and *genuine*. Real, genuine truth and happiness are to be found in Him alone. Others offer a spurious, deceptive, illusory, unreal happiness and joy. In Him alone *true* and *genuine* joy is to be found.

Second, He is called HE THAT HATH THE KEY OF DAVID, HE THAT OPENETH, AND NO MAN SHUTTETH; AND SHUTTETH AND NO MAN OPENETH. This is a quotation from Isaiah 22.22, where it is a description of Eliakim, the faithful steward of Hezekiah. The king had given him the key so that none could gain admission to the royal palace and to the royal presence except through him alone. Jesus is the steward of God; He is the one person who is able to introduce us to the presence and the riches of God.

In verse 8 the Risen Christ says: BEHOLD, I HAVE SET BEFORE THEE AN OPEN DOOR AND NO MAN CAN SHUT IT. There is a great

72

wealth of meaning in this phrase. There are many explanations of it; and we do not need to choose between them, in the sense of choosing one and abandoning the rest. It may well be that all the explanations of it are true.

i. We have already seen that the history of Philadelphia would make us think of the door as *the door of opportunity*. In the old days Philadelphia had been founded to be the missionary of Hellenism to the wilds of Phrygia; and now *the door of missionary opportunity* is open to it. Every one of us has a missionary opportunity. A man who had been touched for Christ came to Spurgeon and asked him what he could do about winning others. Spurgeon asked him: 'What are you? What do you do?' The man said: 'I am an engine-driver.' 'Then,' said Spurgeon, 'is your fireman a Christian?' 'I don't know,' said the man. 'Go back,' said Spurgeon, 'and find out, and start on him.' There is a missionary door for everyone of us, not in Africa or Asia or the islands of the sea, but where we live and work. A man can be a missionary at his day's work.

The door of the opportunity to *self-improvement* is open to everyone of us. Ignorance may be excusable, but neglect of knowledge never is; and there are few places where there are no opportunities to learn about the Bible, to study methods of teaching, to meet together in study and in prayer, to widen out minds and to broaden our knowledge, that we may be better equipped to serve God and our fellowmen.

The door of the opportunity to *service* is open to every one of us. If we are looking for things to do for others, in order to turn our Christianity into something practical, none of us needs to look very far.

ii. It is certain that in Philadelphia there were a great many Jews (Revelation 3.9); and it is certain that many of the Christians had come into Christianity from Judaism. When they were converted, they would find the synagogue door shut in their faces; they would find themselves excommunicated, cursed as apostates and shut out. The Risen Christ is saying to those who had to go through that tragic experience: 'Men may shut you out from their fellowship, but the door to fellowship with me can never be closed on you by any man.'

iii. The door may be none other than *Jesus Himself*. Jesus said 'I am the door' (John 10.7, 9). In the ancient sheepfold there was no gate or door; there was only an opening in the wall through which the sheep passed. When the sheep were all gathered within the fold the shepherd himself lay down across the opening, so that none could get in or out except over him. The shepherd was literally the door. So then Jesus is to us the door to God; through Him we enter in.

iv. The door may be the door of *prayer*. In prayer we have a door which is constantly open, a door which no man can ever shut, a door which leads directly to the presence of God.

The last phrase of this verse says that the Christians of Philadelphia HAVE KEPT CHRIST'S WORD AND HAVE NOT DENIED HIS NAME. The two essentials of the Christian life are *obedience to Christ in action*, and *fearlessness in witness to Him*.

In verse 9 we have a picture of the coming defeat of heathenism and the coming triumph of Christianity. Sometimes in early Christian literature there is a grim savagery in the Christian expectation of the destruction of the enemies of Christ. To Tertullian one of the joys of heaven would be to see the heathen persecutors writhing in hell. 'How vast the spectacle that day, and how wide! What sight shall wake my wonder, what my laughter, my joy and exultation? as I see all those kings, those great kings, welcomed (we are told) in heaven, along with Jove, along with those who told of their ascent, groaning in the depths of darkness! And the magistrates

who persecuted the name of Jesus, liquefying in fiercer flames
than they kindled in their rage against the Christians! Those
sages, too, the philosophers blushing before their disciples as
they blaze together! . . . And then there will be the tragic actors
to be heard, more vocal in their own tragedy; and the players to
be seen, lither of limb by far in the fire; and then the charioteer
to watch, red all over in the wheel of flame; and next the
athletes to be gazed upon, not in their gymnasiums but hurled
in the fire' (*De Spectaculis*, 30; the translation is that of T. R.
Glover in the Loeb Classical Library edition). Such a thirst for
vengeance, and such an expectation of triumph may make us
fastidiously shrink away. But we must remember what the
Christians were going through, the persecution they endured
and the tortures they had to bear. It was inevitable that they
should look for the day when the tables would be turned, when
they would triumph and when their savage persecutors would
be destroyed. This remains true, that the day will come, when
those who refuse the way of Christ will see the error of their
ways, and with their whole hearts will regret their refusal.

In verse 10 it is the promise of the Risen Christ that in the
great day of trial He will keep those who have kept faith with
Him. Eric Liddell was one of Britain's great athletes, and later
he was to become a missionary who was to lay down his life for
Christ. In 1924 he was to run for Britain in the Olympic Games.
It was discovered that the preliminary heats of the hundred
meters race were on a Sunday. Quietly, but definitely, Liddell
said: 'I'm not running.' The day of the four hundred meters
came. As Liddell went to the starting-point an unknown man
slipped a little piece of paper into his hand. Liddell opened it
and read it. It was a text, I Samuel 2.30: 'Them that honor me,
I will honor.' That day Eric Liddell set up a world's record time
for the four hundred meters race; and who will deny that that
slip of paper gave Eric Liddell a strength to run as he had never

run before? Jesus Christ never fails the man who refuses to fail Him.

Verse 10 speaks of THE HOUR OF TEMPTATION WHICH IS TO COME UPON THE WORLD. One of the most basic beliefs of the Jews was their belief in the two ages. There was *This Present Age*, which was wholly bad, and wholly under the sway of evil; there was *The Age to Come*, which would be the golden age of God. In between the two ages there was to come *The Day of the Lord*. That would be a terrible day of judgment, of wrath, of the separation of the good and the bad, and of utter destruction for everything and everyone in this world who was against God. What is meant by this verse is that when the day of reckoning comes, the man who has been faithful will stand the test and win the reward of his fidelity.

In verse 11 the Risen Christ urges the Christians of Philadelphia to see to it that NO MAN TAKES THEIR CROWN. The crown is the crown given to the victorious athlete in the games. The meaning will be clear, if we paraphrase the verse: 'See that you do not forfeit your crown.' No one can ever take our crown from us, but by our own weakness or our own infidelity we ourselves can lose it.

Verse 12 says that he who overcomes will be made A PILLAR IN THE TEMPLE OF MY GOD. We have seen that in Philadelphia one who served the state well was honored with an inscribed pillar in the temple of some god. When a priest had lived and died in holiness and in service, a pillar was added to the temple in his memory. A pillar has one special function. It is the function of a pillar to support the edifice of which it forms a part. If we give all our strength and thought and time and substance to the upbuilding of the Church of Christ, then we too are supports and pillars of the Church. There are two attitudes to the Church. Some people desire to put all they have at the service of the Church; and some people never think of the Church until they want something out of it. Some people desire only to support the Church; and some people desire only that the Church should support them. But the fact remains that the Church can never fully support us until we have given our all to support the Church. We get out of the Church what we bring to it.

This verse goes on to say of the faithful Christian: HE SHALL GO NO MORE OUT. We have already seen that this is a reference to the terrified exodus of the Philadelphians from their city when the earthquakes threatened. It is as if the Risen Christ said: 'The man who is faithful will never need to run away again. He will be able to face anything in the strength which I can give.' Joseph Conrad tells how he was taught by an old sailor to steer a sailing-ship. The old sailor told him that in a storm there was only one thing to do: 'Keep her facing it.' That also is the recipe for the Christian life.

Finally, the Christian is to have THE NEW NAME WRITTEN ON HIM. In the ancient world when a man became a king, or when he became a claimant to a kingdom, the first thing he did was to issue coins with his name stamped upon them. Coinage was the sign of kingship; and the name was the sign of ownership. The Christian is like the coin of God. He ought to have his owner's name stamped upon him. The life of the Christian should be such that all men may see that he is the property of God.

XIII
LAODICAEA

Poverty in Riches

The town of Laodicaea lay forty-three miles south-east of Philadelphia, and about a hundred miles from Ephesus. It was one of a group of three towns which lay in easy sight of each other in the valley of the River Lycus. The two companion towns were Hierapolis and Colosse. Laodicaea was not a very ancient town, for it had been founded in 250 B.C. by Antiochus the Second, and had been called Laodicaea after Antiochus' wife.

Laodicaea had a commanding geographical position. It was situated where the narrow glen of the River Lycus broadens out into the valley of the River Maeander. That narrow glen is the gateway to Phrygia, and it was to command that glen that Laodicaea had originally been built. Laodicaea was a town of great commercial prosperity, for it controlled the trade which flowed down the river valley towards the sea-coast. To add to its importance, there came three great roads to center upon Laodicaea. There came the road from the sea-coast from Attaleia and Perga. There came the road from the north-west which linked her with Philadelphia and Sardis. There came the road from the north-east which came in from Dorylaeum and from Phrygia. Laodicaea's position made her one of the richest commercial centers of the ancient world.

In 133 B.C. Laodicaea became part of the Roman Empire, and it was then that her most spacious days began. The Romans made her an assize town, one of these towns to which the Roman governor periodically came to administer Roman justice. So then, strategically, commercially, and from the point of view of Roman administration, Laodicaea was a most important town.

Laodicaea and the surrounding districts contained a very large number of Jews. As we have said, Laodicaea was founded by Antiochus the Second. Antiochus belonged to the royal house of kings known as the Seleucids. The Seleucids were one of the families amongst whom the empire of Alexander the Great was divided. Now wherever these Seleucids founded a city it was their regular policy to offer free citizenship to all Jews who cared to accept it, for the Jew were useful citizens and brought money and trade to every city in which they settled. Some idea of the number of Jews in Laodicaea and the surrounding districts may be gathered from the following facts. In 62 B.C. Flaccus, the governor of Asia, prohibited the export of currency from his province. The Jews all over the world sent their annual contribution to the Temple at Jerusalem. The Jews defied the ban of Flaccus, and sent their contributions as usual. The gold which they sent was seized as contraband and was found to weigh no less than twenty pounds in weight. Twenty pounds of gold would be equal to about fifteen thousand *drachmae*. One half-shekel was equal to two *drachmae*; there must have been about seven thousand five hundred adult male Jews in Laodicaea and its surrounding district, as well as women and children.

So influential were the Jews in this part of Asia that they could actually bring pressure to bear upon the Roman government. Their influence can be seen in a Roman edict which Josephus cites (*Antiquities of the Jews*, 14.10.20). The Jews had appealed to the Roman governor that they should be granted the right to follow their own customs and to observe their own laws. The local population had protested. The matter had been referred to the Roman consul, and he informed the magistrates of Laodicaea that the Jews were to be allowed to have their special privileges. They were to be allowed to observe their Sabbaths and their ancient rites. The magistrates of Laodicaea accepted the decision, although with an undertone of protest, and wrote back to the governor: 'Although the Trallians there present contradicted them, and were not pleased with these decrees, yet thou didst give order that they should be observed, and informed us that thou hadst been desired to write this to us about them. We, therefore, in obedience to the injunctions which we have received from thee, have received the epistle which thou didst send us, and have laid it up by itself among our public records.' Such was the influence of the Jews in Laodicaea. So many Jews came to live in this part of Asia that even the Jews of Jerusalem were moved to complain about the number of Jews who had forsaken Palestine for the luxuries and the baths of Phrygia.

It is obvious that Christians who lived in a society so permeated with Jewish influence would be in a very difficult position.

There are three sections of this letter which are specially lit up by the local situation in Laodicaea.

i. Laodicaea was a notably wealthy city. It was the center of the banking arrangements of Asia Minor. When Cicero was traveling in the East in 51 B.C. it was in Laodicaea that he cashed his letters of credit. Twice Laodicaea had suffered severely from the ravages of earthquakes. In A.D. 17 it had been devastated by the same earthquake which laid waste Sardis and Philadelphia. At that time it received the same kindness and aid from Tiberius, the Roman Emperor, as these other cities had received. But in A.D. 60 it was again laid waste, and this time, although all aid and assistance was offered, Laodicaea completely refused them, and preferred to rebuild its shattered city out of its own resources. Laodicaea was too rich to accept help from any one. Tacitus, the Roman historian, tells us: 'Laodicaea arose from the ruins by the strength of her own resources, and with no help from us.' As the Risen Christ said, Laodicaea was the city which said: I AM RICH, AND INCREASED WITH GOODS, AND HAVE NEED OF NOTHING (Revelation 3.17). The Laodicaeans were the people who were so well off that they needed help neither from man nor from God. They were the people who believed that money could buy anything; and they had so much of it that they could very well manage without God – so they thought. It is as if the Risen Christ said to Laodicaea: 'You are rich, and you are proud of your riches; but in the things that matter you are poverty-stricken – and you do not know it.'

ii. A very considerable part of the wealth of Laodicaea came from the cloth and the clothing industry. The surrounding countryside was world-famous for a certain breed of black-wooled sheep. Strabo, the ancient geographer, tells us: 'The country around Laodicaea breeds excellent sheep, remarkable not only for the softness of their wool, in which they surpass the Milesian sheep, but for their dark or raven color. The Laodicaeans derive a large part of their revenue from them.' There was a kind of violet, glossy darkness about this wool which made it famous. The Laodicaean factories made at least four different kinds of outer garment which were exported all over the world; and they made one kind of tunic called the *trimita*, which was so famous and so identified with Laodicaea that in later times Laodicaea was sometimes called *Trimitaria*. In face of all this the Risen Christ counsels the Laodicaeans to buy WHITE RAIMENT THAT THOU MAYEST BE CLOTHED, AND THAT THE SHAME OF THY NAKEDNESS DO NOT APPEAR (Revelation 3.18). It is as if the Risen Christ said to the Laodicaeans: 'Your pride is in the clothes which you produce and which you export all over the world, but your soul is naked, and you do not know it.' Laodicaea was the city which thought much of the adornment of the body, and completely forgot the adornment of the soul.

iii. Laodicaea was on the borders of Caria and Phrygia, and one of the most ancient Carian gods was the god Men. Men was the god of healing, and he later came to be identified with Asklepios. Laodicaea was a famous medical school; and in particular it was famous for two kinds of medicine. It was famous for a certain ointment made of nard which was used to cure sore ears. But above all it was famous for a certain eye-powder. The *tephra Phrygia*, the eye-powder of Laodicaea, was world-famous. It was exported in tablet form; and the tablets were ground down and applied to the eyes. This Phrygian powder was held to be a sovereign remedy for weak and ailing eyes. It is in face of this that the Risen Christ counsels the Laodicaeans TO ANOINT THINE EYES WITH EYE-SALVE THAT THOU MAYEST SEE (Revelation 3.18). It is as if the Risen Christ said: 'You are famous all over the world for your eye-salve which can cure weak eyes, but the eyes of your soul are blind, and you do not know it.' Laodicaea was the city which could cure defects of physical sight, but in spiritual sight it was blind. The eye of the body Laodicaea could deal with, but it had never even realized that there was such a thing as the eye of the soul.

There is a strangely modern situation here. The Laodicaeans were the people who put their trust in material prosperity, in outward luxury and in physical health. They put their trust in the things of this world and in the things of time. They tried to build a lasting civilization on material benefits. There is a sense in which that is exactly what the welfare state seeks to do today. It is easy for a state to act on the principle: Give men better housing conditions, better pay, better working conditions; look after their physical health as it has never been looked after before; and then the golden age will dawn; heaven will come upon earth; and all will be well.

We must make no mistake. These things are noble things; these things must be given to men; and the Church must be heart and soul behind every movement which seeks to give them. *But these things are not all.* The man who receives the new house and the new health must also be changed. The aim of Christianity is not so much to change conditions as it is to change men, for if men are changed, the conditions will inevitably be changed; but if men are not changed, the conditions will certainly and inevitably relapse into the old ways or become progressively worse. The Church of Laodicaea stands as a warning to those who remember intensely that man has a body and forget completely that man has a soul. It stands as a warning to those who put their trust in material things, and who leave out God.

XIV
LAODICAEA

The Church of which there was nothing good to say

REVELATION 3.14-22

THE letter to the Church at Laodicaea begins by describing the Risen Christ by two great titles.

i. He is THE AMEN, THE FAITHFUL AND TRUE WITNESS. This strange title THE AMEN may come from either of two sources. It may come from Isaiah 65.16 where God is described as the God of truth, or, it may be, *the God of Amen*. Or, it may come from *Jesus'* custom of prefacing a very serious statement with the words *Verily, verily*, which in Greek are *Amēn, amēn*. This word *Amēn* is a word which was used to affirm and to guarantee a statement as absolutely true and absolutely trustworthy. To say that Jesus is THE AMEN is therefore to say that Jesus is the personification and the affirmation of the truth of God. To begin a letter like this is to begin by saying that what is in it is the truth from God, and that the reader can only neglect the truth at his peril.

ii. He is called THE BEGINNING OF THE CREATION OF GOD. The Greek word for beginning is *archē*, which means *source* and *origin* rather than *beginning*. The one thing that this does not mean is that Jesus was the first thing or person to be created by God. It does mean that Jesus is the source, the origin, the moving cause of all creation. It is another way of saying what John says at the beginning of the Fourth Gospel: 'All things were made by him; and without him was not anything made that was made' (John 1.3). The New Testament is always clear that the God who created the world is also the God who recreates the world; that the God who made all things is also the God who redeems all things.

Verses 15 and 16 go on to say that, because Laodicaea is neither cold nor hot but lukewarm, it will be absolutely and totally rejected; and this is said with such crude violence that the intensity of the feeling behind it cannot be mistaken. The word which is used for *hot* is *zestos*, and *zestos* means more than *hot*; it means *at boiling-point*. Here is the great fact that there can be no real religion without enthusiasm. We have seen that Laodicaea was a great commercial and trading center; we have seen that it was a very prosperous city. It is very likely that the people of Laodicaea drew the line when religion began interfering with their business. G. W. E. Russell tells how, after hearing an evangelical sermon, Viscount Melbourne made the famous remark: 'Things have come to a pretty pass when religion is allowed to invade the sphere of private life.' A decent respectability was all right and even much to be desired, but a religion which was like a fire in a man's bones, and which pervaded every part and corner of his life, was a different thing altogether. There is such a thing as a kind of common-sense religion. The Ten Commandments are doubtless very proper, but when it comes to an enthusiasm which demands that we should love our enemies, and give our goods to the poor, and pray for the people who insult us – that is a very different matter. Laodicaea is condemned because she preferred a respectable morality to a passionate religion.

The word for *lukewarm* is *chliaros*, which means *tepid*. In the district around Laodicaea there were hot mineral springs. A medicinal spring can have a most nauseating taste. It may well be that the picture is taken from these mineral springs, and that the Risen Christ is saying: 'Sometimes when a man goes to drink of the medicinal springs, the tepid and the ill-tasting water makes his gorge rise and makes him want to vomit; that is the way in which I feel about a Church that is neither hot nor cold.' The plain fact is that in Christianity there is no room for neutrality. The person who has not declared for Christ has declared against Christ. The very phrase *a lukewarm Christian* is a contradiction in terms, for a lukewarm Christian has no claim to be called a Christian at all.

Verses 17 and 18 are written against the background for which Laodicaea was famous. It was famous for its wealth; it was famous for its clothing industry; it was famous for its eye-powder. The story of Laodicaea was a success story. The whole attitude of Laodicaea was that it could cope with life quite well by itself. That is no uncommon attitude. So long as things go well men think that they can do without God. But let a disastrous war involve a nation and the men who do not ever pray flock to church to observe national days of prayer. Let death come to a house, and the people in it who have sat very loosely to the Church want the Church and the comfort that the prayers of the Church can bring. It is the lesson of life that there are certain experiences from which it takes God to rescue a man; and it is the experience of life that these things come to every man sooner or later. And when they do come, not all the money in the world can enable a man to deal with them by himself.

In this world there are always two points of view – the human and the divine. From the purely human standpoint a man may be a very successful man; and from the divine point of view he may be a complete failure. There is an old story of a wealthy and selfish woman who died and reached heaven. She was told that she would be taken to the house which had been prepared for her. She passed many beautiful mansions and saw in them people whom in this world she had known and despised. Finally on the very outskirts and suburbs of heaven she was shown a very small and undistinguished house and was told that it was hers. She complained and protested, but she was told quietly: 'That is all we could do for you with the materials you sent up.' In this world it is easy for a man to enrich his life with material things, and at the same time to impoverish his soul. He can forget that he has got a soul, and discover too late that his soul is the part of him which matters most of all. As the Spanish proverb grimly has it: There are no pockets in a shroud.

In verse 19 the Risen Christ says: AS MANY AS I LOVE, I REBUKE AND CHASTEN. It is always the best athlete who is given the hardest training, and the finest student who is set the most demanding tasks. Jerome once remarked that the greatest anger of God is when God withdraws His anger from us. If God ever abandons a man, that man must be bad indeed. No man should ever despise or resent the chastening disciplines of life; he should regard them as a compliment.

The Risen Christ goes on to summon the people of Laodicaea TO BE ZEALOUS AND REPENT. From the strict point of view these two commands should be reversed, for the repentance must come first. The tenses are significant. *Repent* is the *aorist* imperative, and the aorist demands one definitive action. *Be zealous* is the *present* imperative, and the present demands continuous activity. It is as if the Risen Christ was saying: 'Make your decision, and then all your life go on showing your zeal.' There can be no real zeal until the moment of decision has been reached and accepted; and the moment of decision is no real decision unless it is followed by a life of loving, passionate service of Christ and of our fellowmen.

In verse 20 the Risen Christ says: BEHOLD I STAND AT THE DOOR AND KNOCK. There are two possible thoughts here.

i. It may mean that the end is near, and that the new age is about to dawn (cp. Mark 13.29; James 5.9). The early Church was dominated by the thought of the Second Coming; and this may be a summons to be ready before the King and Judge arrives upon the earth. It is always true that eternity is knocking at the door of time.

ii. More likely the thought is that Jesus Christ is knocking at the door of our hearts, because He wishes us to receive Him as our guest. R. H. Charles makes the beautiful suggestion that the words come from the love song of the Song of Solomon: 'It is the voice of my beloved that knocketh saying, Open to me, my sister, my love, my dove' (Song of Solomon 5.2). It is the picture of Christ, the lover of the souls of men, knocking at the door of the human heart. There are certain things which we must note here.

The appeal of Christ is an *individual* appeal. He says: IF ANY MAN HEARS MY VOICE ... I WILL COME IN TO HIM. The appeal of Jesus Christ is not to the Church at large; it is to the heart of every individual man.

The promise of Christ to the man who opens the door of his heart is: I WILL SUP WITH HIM. There is a point here which the English translation does not make. To us *supper* is not a main meal. The Greek ate three meals in the day. *Breakfast* (*akratisma*) was only a slice of dry bread dipped in wine. *Lunch* (*ariston*) was seldom eaten at home; it was a scratch meal eaten in a city square or wherever a man happened to be. But supper (*deipnon*) was the main meal of the day. This was the meal at which a man sat and talked for long, for now there was time, for work was ended. There is something very lovely here. It is not a mere courtesy visit, paid in the passing, which Jesus Christ offers to us. He desires to come in and to sit long with us, and to wait as long as we wish Him to wait. As Henry Lyte wrote in his great hymn:

> Not a brief glance, I beg, a passing word;
> But as Thou dwell'st with Thy disciples, Lord,
> Familiar, condescending, patient, free,
> Come, not to sojourn, but abide with me.

That is precisely what Jesus Christ offers us. He offers us no rushed visit in the passing, but a lingering of His presence without haste.

But He will not force an entry; He stands at the door and knocks. When Holman Hunt drew his great picture of Jesus, the Light of the World, knocking at the door of the human heart, he was right when he pictured that door with no handle on the outside, for the door of the human heart must always be opened from within.

Verse 21 closes with the promise of *victory*. Not only does Christ offer us His presence in the intimate loneliness of our own hearts; He offers us His presence in the battle of life's everyday, that we may emerge from it, not conquered, but conquering.

INDEXES

(*b*) SCRIPTURE PASSAGES

(c) GREEK WORDS